THE
FUTURE
of
THE
NOVEL

For Akin

THE
FUTURE
of
THE
NOVEL

Simon Okotie

MELVILLE HOUSE UK
LONDON

THE FUTURE OF THE NOVEL

First published in 2025 by
Melville House UK
Suite 2000
16/18 Woodford Road
London E7 0HA

and

Melville House Publishing
46 John Street
Brooklyn, NY 112001

mhpbooks.com   @melvillehouse

A CIP catalogue record for this book is available from the British Library

UK: 978-1-911545-75-0
US: 978-1-685891-61-9

1 3 5 7 9 10 8 6 4 2

Printed in Denmark by Nørhaven, Viborg
Typesetting by Roland Codd

Chronology

The future of the novel is inevitably rooted in its past. If, as argued here, the novel has started self-reflectively thinking itself into existence, then the first systematic theory about it provides the starting point for that history. This future starts, then, with 'arguably the founder of the theory of the novel as a field' (Timothy Bewes in *Free Indirect: The Novel in a Postfictional Age*): the Hungarian literary theorist and philosopher Georg Lukács.

1914–15
Lukács wrote the first draft of his *The Theory of the Novel* in the summer of 1914; the final version was written in the winter of 1914–15. The outbreak of the war provided Lukács' 'immediate motive for writing'

the book. It was originally intended to be written as a
series of dialogues between a group of young people
who had withdrawn from 'the war psychosis of their
environment' to engage in a series of conversations
as a means of trying to deepen their understanding of
themselves and each other before gradually moving
to address their 'outlook on a Dostoevskian world.'
While Lukács subsequently dropped this plan for
the book, it was nevertheless 'written in a mood of
permanent despair over the state of the world.'

It is unsurprising that the first great theorists of
the novel as a formalised field of study emerged in
the wake of the Great War. This was a time in which
the '[o]ld forms no longer held', a period during
which writers alive to their times 'could not pre-
sume upon common worldviews, common values,
or the kinds of stability that make the fiction of the
nineteenth century at once various and universal'
(Michael Schmidt in *The Novel: A Biography*).

10 April 1919
'Modern Novels', an unsigned *Times Literary
Supplement* essay by Virginia Woolf, criticises the
work of the novelists H. G. Wells, Arnold Bennett
and John Galsworthy for its failure to capture 'the
essential thing': life, spirit, truth or reality. 'If we tried

to formulate our meaning in one word we should say that these three writers are materialists, and for that reason have disappointed us and left us with the feeling that the sooner English fiction turns its back upon them, as politely as may be, and marches, if only into the desert, the better for its soul.'

3 September 1919

Art and Answerability – the earliest known publication by the Soviet literary theorist Mikhail Bakhtin – appears in a provincial Russian journal.

1920

The Theory of the Novel is published.

1922

'In the spring 1922 issue of the avant-garde American literary journal *Little Review*, Ezra Pound published a calendar for a modern era. The months were renamed after Greek and Roman deities, under the heading "Year 1 p.s.U". Readers in tune with literary innovations knew that those letters stood for "post scriptum *Ulysses*", or "after the writing of *Ulysses*". With the publication of James Joyce's novel in February 1922, on the author's fortieth birthday, a new age had begun. Pound (his most famous slogan:

"Make It New") was a great one for announcing, or demanding, literary revolutions; this time history would vindicate him. A century on, 1922 still looks like the year literature changed, when modernism came into its own. It was the year not only of *Ulysses*, but also "The Waste Land", by the thirty-four-year-old T.S. Eliot, first published in October. The great novel of modernism was followed by its greatest single poem. These would be enough to mark 1922 as a watershed. But in this year too, Virginia Woolf, the same age as Joyce, published *Jacob's Room*, her first radically experimental novel, and began writing *Mrs Dalloway*.' (From '1922: the year that made modernism' by John Mullan, *New Statesman*.)

Modernism is a 'comprehensive but vague term' (according to *The Penguin Dictionary of Literary Terms and Literary Theory*) for literature that breaks free from conventions, forms and traditions; provides fresh perspectives on our place and purpose in the universe; or experiments with form and style. It is concerned, in particular, 'with language and how to use it' – and with writing itself.

March 1923

Arnold Bennett's article 'Is the Novel Decaying' is published. In it, he cites *Jacob's Room* as characteristic of what the new novelists are doing. Bennett had 'seldom read a cleverer book ... It is packed and bursting with originality, and it is exquisitely written. But the characters do not vitally survive in the mind because the author has been obsessed by details of originality and cleverness.'

18 May 1924
'Mr Bennett and Mrs Brown' (published as 'Character in Fiction') – a paper in response to Bennett's article – is read by Woolf to 'the Heretics' at Girton College, Cambridge.

14 May 1925
Woolf's *Mrs Dalloway* is published.

January–March 1927
E. M. Forster's *Aspects of the Novel* is given as a series of lectures at Trinity College, Cambridge.

April 1927
The 'Opening Pages of a Work in Progress' (*Finnegans Wake*) by James Joyce appear in the literary journal *transition*.

5 May 1927

Woolf's *To the Lighthouse* is published.

20 October 1927

Forster's *Aspects of the Novel* is published.

24 December 1928

Bakhtin is arrested as part of a campaign to terrorise and repress Soviet intellectuals. This was aimed not just at independent intellectuals such as himself but also at those friendly to the regime who were advocating different lines to those recently adopted by the Communist Party (according to Ken Hirschkop's *The Cambridge Introduction to Mikhail Bakhtin* – the source of much of the remaining Bakhtin chronology below).

June 1929

Bakhtin's *Problems of Dostoevsky's Creative Art* is published. The book is praised by the head of the Commissariat of Enlightenment, Anatoly Lunacharsky. It is crucial that he has friends and advocates willing to defend him, 'even within the ranks of the Bolsheviks.'

22 July 1929

Bakhtin is sentenced to five years in the Solovki labour camp. Given his poor health – chronic osteomyelitis as well as earlier bouts of tuberculosis and meningitis – this is 'tantamount to a death sentence for him.' His wife Elena and his friend Mariia Iudina know Maxim Gorky's wife Ekatarina; they persuade her to ask Gorky to intervene.

22 February 1930
Gorky's telegrams to the OGPU (the forerunner of the KGB) pay off: Bakhtin's sentence is reduced to 'internal exile'.

29 March 1930
Bakhtin moves, with Elena, to Kustanai in Kazakhstan to serve his sentence.

1930-36
Bakhtin composes *Discourse in the Novel*. His considerable although largely unacknowledged debt to Lukács was incurred between the mid-1920s and the early 1940s, a period in which Lukács became central to Marxist social thought, gaining, in the 1930s, 'the reputation of a serious player, and indeed of a canon-maker, in the emerging field of institutionalised Marxist aesthetics.' Bakhtin's intellectual career, meanwhile, evolved far from official circles: by the time of his key polemics with Lukács in the

1930s he had been almost forgotten. This meant that Bakhtin's opportunities for voicing his own position were, at this time, 'largely confined to a silent dialogue with his opponent.' (Galin Tihanov in *The Master and the Slave – Lukács, Bakhtin, and the Ideas of their Time*.)

27 March 1931
Arnold Bennett dies. Woolf describes him as lovable and genuine in her diary the following day: 'Queer how one regrets the dispersal of anybody who seemed – as I say – genuine: who had direct contact with life – for he abused me; and I yet rather wished him to go on abusing me; and me abusing him. An element in life – even in mine that was so remote – taken away. This is what one minds.'

February – June 1932
Samuel Beckett composes a large part of his novel *Dream of Fair to Middling Women*, in Paris.

14 October 1940
Bakhtin delivers the lecture 'Discourse in the Novel' at the Gorky Institute. It is published under the title 'From the Prehistory of Novelistic Discourse'.

24 March 1941

Bakhtin delivers the lecture 'The Novel as a Literary Genre' at the Gorky Institute. It is published under the title 'Epic and Novel'.

Summer 1945

Beckett has a 'vision' in his mother's room that decisively changes the trajectory of his work: 'I realised that Joyce had gone as far as one could in the direction of knowing more, [being] in control of one's material. He was always adding to it; you only have to look at his proofs to see that. I realised that my own way was in impoverishment, in lack of knowledge and in taking away, in subtracting rather than in adding.' (James Knowlson, *Damned to Fame: the Life of Samuel Beckett.*)

25 October 1951

Jack Kerouac meets his friend Ed White for supper in a Chinese restaurant on New York City's 124th street. White had been sketching the city's buildings in little architectural notebooks (according to Kerouac's biographer Gerald Nicosia), and he suggested that Kerouac should try 'sketching with words' in his own notebooks.

Summer 1972

Ishmael Reed's novel *Mumbo Jumbo* is published.

1973

'When Thomas Pynchon published his first novels in the early- and mid-1960s, nobody called them postmodern, for the very good reason that the term barely existed at that time. If anyone felt the need to categorise them, perfectly suitable categories were available: *V.* (1963) and *The Crying of Lot 49* (1966) were satires, or perhaps examples of black humour. By the mid-1980s, Pynchon had been canonised as the very model of a postmodernist, and *Gravity's Rainbow* (1973) in particular, his third book, as the definitive postmodern novel.' *Thomas Pynchon in Context* by Inger H. Dalsgaard (ed.).

'Postmodernism' is, for *The Penguin Dictionary of Literary Terms and Literary Theory*, a general and sometimes controversial term. Its features (in relation to the novel) include parody, pastiche, eclecticism and writing based on chance.

1988

Henry Louis Gates Jr.'s *The Signifying Monkey: A Theory of African-American Literary Criticism* is published. Gates charts the intertextual relationship between Reed's 'postmodern' novel *Mumbo Jumbo*, Richard Wright's 'realism' – in novels such as *Native Son* (1940) and *Black Boy* (1945) – and Ralph Ellison's 'modernism' – in *Invisible Man* (1952), for instance. Gates relates these types of formal relationships to Bakhtin's concept of 'double-voiced discourse'.

30 September 2003

J. M. Coetzee's *Elizabeth Costello* is published.

14 September 2014, 29 September, 2016 and 5 June 2018

Publication of Rachel Cusk's: *Outline*; *Transit*; and *Kudos*.

10 October 2019, 7 October 2020 and 8 September 2021

Publication of Jon Fosse's: *The Other Name: Septology I-II*; *I is Another: Septology III-V*; and *A New Name: Septology VI-VII*.

26 July 2022

Timothy Bewes' *Free Indirect: The Novel in a Postfictional Age* is published. It opens with a quote from Cusk in which she says, 'I'm not interested in character because I don't think character exists anymore.' Bewes goes on to argue that *Elizabeth Costello* illustrates a new mode of thought that has become strikingly apparent in English-language fiction in the two decades since its publication. Bewes calls this 'postfiction: an element in the practice of fiction that unthinks or deauthorises the very claims made by the work'.

19 August 2023

Alex Reisner publishes an article in *The Atlantic* identifying authors whose copyrighted works are being used to train large language (AI) models.

20 September 2023

The US Authors Guild files a class-action lawsuit against OpenAI in New York City.

25 September 2023

The Atlantic publishes a searchable version of the database that Reisner had used to identify the copyrighted works.

27 September 2023

The US Authors Guild publishes guidance in response to the publication of Reisner's database.

5 October 2023

Jon Fosse wins the Nobel Prize in Literature.

13 March 2024

The European Parliament adopts the Artificial Intelligence Act – the world's first major set of regulatory ground rules governing AI.

Futures Past: An Introduction

John Carruthers' *Scheherazade, or the Future of the English Novel* was published in 1927 as part of Kegan Paul's 'To-Day and To-Morrow' series. Arguing that self-analysis had begun to dominate the form, the essay (which should, perhaps, have been subtitled 'the future of the novel *in* English') called James Joyce's *Ulysses* 'a colossal failure to be the masterpiece of our day and generation', the main reason being that Joyce believed so completely in chaos that he tried to represent it, rather than finding a form for resolving the chaos into order. The fiction of this period fell short of the highest standards, for Carruthers, partly due to the prevailing spiritual conditions in the wake of the Great War and partly through the confusing scientific and literary influences acting upon novelists in this post-war period.

The 'psychological influence' was the first and most important of these. Deriving from several sources, both literary and scientific, it served, through the later works of Henry James, for instance, to 'virtually abolish' the story, reducing events to a bare minimum, the characters concerning themselves with minute analyses of inner consciousness. Another influence on the novel in English at this time was that of Dostoevsky and Tolstoy, who, for Carruthers, were the two greatest 'psychological novelists' in European literature. This, though, dealt another blow to form and plot, with formless 'slices of life' becoming fashionable, as did an interest, largely due to Dostoevsky, in what Carruthers thought of as abnormal, morbid or pathological states of mind. Then came the 'flood of psychoanalysis' which, for Carruthers, muddied the waters further.

The trend, then, in European fiction at this time was away from objectivity and towards increasingly minute and analytic explorations of inner life, with the 'growing points' in the contemporary prose fiction to be found, in particular, in the work of Virginia Woolf, who Carruthers took to be the most important post-war novelist writing in English. But it was Joyce who, for Carruthers, had carried this interiorising tendency as far as it apparently could go, and 'that is to say, considerably farther than it can go with safety'.

Carruthers' is perhaps the least well-known example of what literary scholar Peter Boxall calls a 'procession of essays by working novelists on the future of the novel': from Henry James's 'The Future of the Novel' (1899), to D. H. Lawrence's 'The Future of the Novel' (1923), Arnold Bennett's 'Is the Novel Decaying?' (1926), Alain Robbe-Grillet's 'A Future for the Novel' (1956), William Burroughs' 'The Future of the Novel' (1964), Anaïs Nin's *The Novel of the Future* (1968), Zadie Smith's 'Two Paths for the Novel' (2008) and China Miéville's 'The Future of the Novel' (2012). Of all of these, Carruthers' is the essay that was published in argu-ably the most interesting and innovative year for the form (in English). It was not only the year in which Woolf's *To the Lighthouse* was published and within which Joyce's 'Opening Pages of a Work in Progress' (eventually published as *Finnegans Wake*) appeared in the Paris literary journal *transition*, but the year in which E. M. Forster gave an influential series of lectures at Trinity College, Cambridge, published, as *Aspects of the Novel*, around the same time as

Carruthers' essay. In addition, Woolf provided her own prognostications in 'Poetry, Fiction and the Future', a lecture delivered to the Oxford University English Club and published later that year in the *New York Herald Tribune*.

Some of the volumes in 'To-day and To-morrow' – the great-grandparent of, and inspiration for, the present series – were paired as a means of 'taking opposing or at least contrasting positions on some topics' (according to Max Saunders' survey of the series in his book *Imagined Futures*). The intention was to recreate the atmosphere and drama of the debating chamber from which the series emerged: founded by the brains behind 'To-day and To-morrow', C. K. Ogden (and others), in 1909, the Heretics Society was, for Saunders, 'the most prominent forum for public intellectuals to speak at in Cambridge'. The dialectical format is reflected in the series from the outset, with the scientist J. B. S. Haldane's 'coruscating paper' delivered to the Heretics on 4 February 1923 and published, probably in late 1923, as *Daedalus; or, Science and the Future*, a small hardback pocket-book of ninety-three pages whose 'buoyant utopian advocacy' was pitted against the 'cynical caution' of Bertrand Russell's *Icarus, or, The Future of Science* (1924). The former's optimism about 'the potential of science to enhance human reproduction or devise new fuel economies' was countered by the latter's pessimism 'about how power will use and misuse such knowledges'.

Scheherazade was not paired at the time of the original series; the present essay is an attempt to fill this gap, with the benefit of nearly a century's hindsight, and primarily as a means of finding a way into an otherwise dauntingly broad and deep topic. It is, then, a conversation (and, at times, a disputation) with Carruthers, particularly in relation (from our contemporary standpoint) to the fact that, despite writing at a time – five years after the publication of *Ulysses* and two after *Mrs Dalloway* – that was, in retrospect, a golden era for the novel in English, he asserts that 'the indubitable masterpiece of English post-war fiction' was still to be written. What, precisely, could he have been looking for? And what does this mean, now, for the future of the form?

It is a dialogue between novelists rather than theorists, although it draws heavily on literary theory in the course of the conversation. It uses aspects of theory not as a means of fashioning and defending an academic case but as a basis for tracing a possible trajectory for the future of what used to be called the discipline of novel-writing but which is now more commonly referred to as novelistic 'practice'. It relies, in particular, on those theorists who chime with a lived experience of the practicalities (and possibilities) of novel-writing, and what that entails is a strong reliance on the twentieth-century Soviet theorist Mikhail Bakhtin. This is not just because he is 'the mythologically powerful ancestor of current schools of thought' on the novel (as intellectual historian Galin Tihanov describes him), 'the lonely Russian genius' who, chronically ill, was forced into exile and whose intellectual career evolved in obscurity (unlike his contemporary and 'rival', Georg Lukács, author of *The Theory of the Novel*), but because he is the theorist whose understanding of the novel is almost unerringly, uncannily precise and prescient.

The decrepit novelistic apparatus of setting, plot and character – as well as the nature of the novelist themselves – provide the main structure for the essay; I also provide an idiosyncratic chronology and a 'further reading' list that contains no novels. The structure is underpinned by reflections on the unfolding of my own formative novelistic failings – in a manner similar to that of the narrator of Mario Levrero's *The Luminous Novel*: a novel that is mainly about the failure to write a novel.

All of which assumes, of course, that the novel *has* a future, and this in the context of the seemingly perennial debates about the decline – or even demise – of the form. Henry James, for one, was optimistic – the novel would endure, for him, as long as life continued to project itself onto the imagination, with nothing yet discovered that is better suited to this purpose. The only thing that would result in the novel's total functional failure, for James, would be 'some grave fault in some high quarter'. Yet, even then, might fiction not 'find a second wind, or a fiftieth, in the very portrayal of that collapse?'

We are better, then, more immediately to concern ourselves, as James did, with seeing that this 'image in the mirror' continues to be vivid and various. And the place to start remains the concerns of those who feel the novel to be 'considerably menaced', those who 'see the whole business as too divorced on the one side from observation and perception, and on the other from the art and taste' of the form, those who 'get too little of the first-hand impression, the effort to penetrate ... and still less, if possible, of any science of composition, any architecture, distribution, proportion'. The place to start, in other words, is with the building blocks of perception itself and with their mysterious transmutation into words on the page.

A Fortunate Failure: Architectonics as a Setting for the Future

'Art begins not with flesh but with the house.' (Deleuze and Guattari in *What is Philosophy?*) That is why, for them (as for philosophers such as Schopenhauer), 'architecture is the first of the arts'. Architecture's 'interlocking of differently orientated frames' – whether walls or floors, mirrors, doors or windows – are on this basis 'imposed on the other arts' (including the novel) as a means of both holding the 'compound of created sensations' that constitute the artwork and, through breaking their bounds, allowing it to 'stand up on its own' – which is to say, of enabling the artwork to become a 'monument', and one that, far from being inert, will live, breathe and lead a life of its own.

Deleuze and Guattari dwell, in particular, on Proust, since he, 'more than anyone', made these two elements – of framing sensations and allowing them to live – 'almost follow one another'. This is exemplified in the hypnagogic opening of *À la recherche du temps perdu* when the narrator wakes in the middle of the night, not knowing where he is, not even being sure, at first, of *who* he is: his body, 'still too heavy with sleep to move, would endeavour to construe from the pattern of its tiredness the position of its various limbs, in order to deduce therefrom the direction of the wall, the location of the furniture, to piece together and give a name to the house in which it lay'. The body's 'composite memory' would then offer up 'a whole series of rooms in which it had at one time or another slept, while the unseen walls, shifting and adapting themselves to the shape of each successive room that it remembered, whirled round it in the dark' (in the classic Scott Moncrieff/ Kilmartin translation of the novel). Here, then, is an as it were concrete albeit shifting example of how, in Proust (for Deleuze and Guattari), '[e]verything begins with [h]ouses, each of which must join up its sections and hold up compounds', with Proust conjuring extraordinary 'beings of flight' from these architectural interfaces.

Elizabeth Grosz's restatement and elaboration of this Deleuze/Guattari thesis (in *Chaos, Territory,*

Art: Deleuze and the Framing of the Earth) is that 'the first gesture of art is not, as Nietzsche believed, the transformation of flesh and blood' into canvas, oil or narrative: instead, it is 'the construction or fabrication of the frame'. This, in turn, requires a more primary – and perhaps even primal – gesture: that of separating the body from nature and from its world to enable sensation to autonomously detach itself from its creator and perceiver. Only then can 'something of the chaos from which it is drawn . . . breathe and have a life of its own'. Enabling the compound of sensations to 'stand up' in this way is, for Deleuze and Guattari, 'the only law of creation'; it also represents, for them, '[t]he artist's greatest difficulty'.

Reading Jack Kerouac is a cliché of a man's early twenties. I'd studied engineering rather than literature and was working for a consultancy in Cavendish Square before Kerouac's 'spontaneous prose', the bebop descendant of Joyce's jazz age 'stream of consciousness', brought me to *Ulysses*, led me to quit my job and took me on the road, initially to the Barri de la Ribera district of Barcelona, where I stayed in the apartment of a friend of a friend of mine who was

known in our circle as Clare-with-the-hair. I took
Kerouac's Joyce-inspired experimental novel *Visions
of Cody*, with its impressionistic word-sketches of a
post-war New York City, as a blueprint, somewhat
self-consciously, for living the life of a novelist, and
started trying to 'sketch' the view through the apartment's north-facing rear window.

What I was trying to capture – aside, that is, from
an accurate correspondence to what my mind and
senses were perceiving – was a *totality*. I wasn't just
interested in a snapshot: I wanted, in my naïveté, to
capture *everything*. I wanted and expected, in other
words, to discover a method in my 'sketching' not
only of reflecting reality but of somehow *encompassing* it in its entirety, at least for that fleeting
moment. Yet almost immediately the more-or-less
static scene defeated me, perhaps because I had mis-
taken what Elizabeth Grosz calls 'the repetition of
sensations already experienced or available' for that
compound of sensations 'generated and proliferated
only by art'. I would now describe this (using the
title of a work by the novelist Georges Perec) as
an attempt at exhausting a place – an attempt at
writing a spontaneous novel recording everything
that passed through my field of vision – transposed
from Paris to Barcelona. It was one that, in my case,

went absolutely nowhere, for the simple reason that I had misunderstood something fundamental about the nature of the novel.

꞉ ꞉ ꞉ ꞉ ꞉ ꞉

Henry James deploys an architectural metaphor to argue (in his preface to *The Portrait of a Lady*) for the novel's extraordinary variety, vividness and plasticity. The 'house of fiction' has, for James, not one window but a million: the number of possible windows is, in fact, beyond reckoning. What pierces the vast architectural façade is the 'individual vision' of each novelist and the 'pressure' that their individual will exerts upon it. Even though these apertures 'hang so, all together, over the human scene', each is different in shape and size to all of the others, resulting in a greater dissimilarity 'of report' than might have been expected. At each window stands a figure surveying the scene with 'a field glass' – an instrument unique to each such individual. This is what ensures the distinctiveness of each observer's impressions of the scene. The field of vision is, for James, each novelist's subject-matter, with each window – whether broad and balconied or low-lintelled and narrow – being their literary form. These are nothing, though, when compared to 'the posted presence of the watcher', which James equates with the artist's consciousness.

Such apertures are also, though, 'mere holes in a dead wall' – they are not (as I had naïvely intimated) swing doors opening straight onto life; there is, in short, a discontinuity between the two sides of the façade. At the same time, however – as Carruthers indicates – 'there is no hard and fast division' between them: London on a summer's day is not 'the virtual hero' of Woolf's *Mrs Dalloway* (as it is with New York, for Carruthers, in John dos Passos' 1925 novel *Manhattan Transfer*); it is though, still crucial, with the characters of Clarissa, Peter Walsh, Lucrezia Warren Smith and Doris Kilman emerging from it and fading into it again. How, then, does such framing produce a 'compound of created sensations' that might eventually 'stand up on its own'? How, further, does it capture something whole or total, rather than something that is partial or incomplete? Georg Lukács' answer to the second question – and Mikhail Bakhtin's response to it – suggest both a possible approach to the first question and a potential route towards the future.

❘ ❭ ❭ ▶ ▶ ▶

The primary focus of discussion in *The Theory of the Novel* is the contrast between the epic and the novel, with Lukács arguing for the latter as 'the epic of an age in which the extensive totality of life is no longer directly given'. While acknowledging that our world, having become 'infinitely large . . . is richer in gifts and dangers than the world of the Greeks', Lukács argues that 'such wealth cancels out the positive meaning – the totality – upon which their life was based.' Here totality is 'world-embracing', implying something that is closed within itself and which, for that reason, is capable of completion since everything occurs within it: 'nothing is excluded from it and nothing points at a higher reality outside it'; everything ripens within it 'to its own perfection'. Such a world-embracing totality is no longer available to us: '[a] totality that can be simply accepted is no longer given to the forms of art' – it was lost in antiquity. The modern novelist is thus faced with two possibilities if they wish to carry the world's fragmentary nature into 'the world of forms': they must either reduce, undermine and destabilise their material until they are able to encompass it, or they must demonstrate 'polemically' the impossibility of achieving their aim while exposing 'the inner nullity of their own means'.

Lukács later built on his own position to argue for 'critical realism' as a key purpose of the novel – 'an artistic cognition of reality, which would show the actual workings of the social structure beneath surface appearances', in Bakhtin scholar Ken Hirschkop's loose definition. The eventual purpose of Lukács' project of totality in the novel in the mid-1930s was, then (for Hirschkop), to 'penetrate the mystifying appearance of capitalist society by totalising its elements, revealing the profound interconnectedness that made capitalism systemic'. Capitalism was, for Lukács, essentially fragmented, appearing as a series of multiple strands connecting people and commodities, from the extraction of raw materials, through manufacturers and retailers to consumers. The only way of revealing the system's true nature was to 'join up the dots': to show how the parts of the system were intimately connected with each other. The novel of critical realism shared, in this respect, the aspirations of the classical epic, though these aspirations were more difficult to realise given the challenges of representing this particular totality – the integrated character of capitalist society – which was, for Lukács, inherently fractured and contradictory.

Bakhtin's response, in his 'Epic and Novel: Toward a Methodology for the Study of the Novel' (to give it its full title), was what Galin Tihanov calls a 'manifesto work' delivered as a paper to the Gorky Institute of World Literature in 1941. An entry in a notebook containing 'Working materials on the theory of the novel' from the late 1930s or early 1940s signals something of Bakhtin's intentions with this lecture. In it, Bakhtin characterises Lukács' position, in essence, as one in which it is 'the features of the depicted ["Homeric"] order' that differentiate the epic from the novel – that something in the *actual* past made the epic possible. Bakhtin's view is that this position, rooted as it is in the thought of Hegel, is 'flawed by naïve realism'. Instead, the epic depicts 'a world *projected* into the past, on to the distanced plane of memory' (emphasis added); yet this is not a 'real' past that is tied to the present by the unfolding of history – it is, instead, a 'valorised past of beginnings and peak times' in a nation's history, one that is 'distanced, finished and closed like a circle'. This 'absolute epic distance' is contrasted with the 'contemporaneity' of the novel, within which the present 'is essentially and in principle unfinished: according to its very essence it demands continuation, it moves into the future, and the more actively and consciously it moves forward into this future, the more tangible and essential is its unfinishedness'.

Bakhtin's paper argued, in short, for a position that was quite at odds with that held by many of his contemporaries, including Lukács (according to Hirschkop), 'that the Soviet novel should be like a new epic'. Yet still he couldn't mention Lukács by name. It is not that Lukács' writing couldn't – or didn't – at this time become the target of open disagreement (according to Tihanov); it was just that such contention was reserved for 'comrades who were considered loyal enough to compete for the honourable (or, under Stalin, merely life-saving) title of true believers.' As someone burdened by prior political trials and 'enforced isolation', Bakhtin was in no position to participate openly in such polemics.

᠈ ᠈ ᠈ ᠈ ᠈ ᠈

A parallel disagreement – about the past, the novel's present-tense perspective and its connection with an idealised future – was transpiring within the quite different context of English letters during this period: between 'several young writers' (to use a phrase of Woolf's in relation to Joyce) and their pre-war predecessors. Arnold Bennett, in particular, was 'probably the best-known English novelist of the time' (according to literary scholar Samuel Hynes) and it was Woolf, according to Carruthers, who 'most openly expressed the reaction against the [latter's] sociological methods'. While accepting Bennett's view that character is the foundation of good fiction, Woolf weighed in against the huge emphasis that English pre-war novelists had placed upon 'the fabric of things'. Instead of looking at life and at human nature in the form of the person beside them, she said, these writers had 'looked very powerfully, searchingly, and sympathetically out of the window': at factories within which women 'make twenty-five dozen earthenware pots every day', their employers 'smoking rich cigars while the nightingale sings' (in the case of John Galsworthy); or at utopias 'where there are public nurseries, fountains, and libraries, dining-rooms, drawing-rooms, and marriages; where every citizen is generous and candid, manly and magnificent, and rather like [the author] himself' (in the case of H. G. Wells). Woolf cites in particular the case of Bennett's novel *Hilda Lessways*, quoting from it at length):

The bailiwick of Turnhill lay behind her; and all the murky district of the Five Towns, of which Turnhill is the northern outpost, lay to the south. At the foot of Chatterley Wood the canal wound in large curves on its way towards the undefiled

plains of Cheshire and the sea. On the canal-side,
exactly opposite to Hilda's window, was a flour-
mill, that sometimes made nearly as much smoke
as the kilns and the chimneys closing the prospect
on either hand. From the flour-mill a bricked path,
which separated a considerable row of new cottages
from their appurtenant gardens, led straight into
Lessways Street, in front of Mrs Lessways' house.
By this path Mr Skellorn should have arrived, for
he inhabited the farthest of the cottages.

These writers had, in short, 'given us a house in
the hope that we may be able to deduce the human
beings who live there'. Woolf felt that, in order to
complete their books, 'it seem[ed] necessary to do
something – to join a society, or, more desperately,
to write a cheque.' And while they helped make
that house a much better place within which to live,
they had also set about it in entirely the wrong way.
Novels are, after all, primarily (for Woolf) about
people, and only in a subsidiary sense about the
houses they live in.

Carruthers refers in his essay to a lecture Woolf
delivered at Girton College, Cambridge, in May
1924. Yet using that as a starting point is, for Hynes,
like 'like watching the third round of a fifteen-round

fight'. Although not strictly speaking the start of
the quarrel, the document Hynes identifies as the
first in the caseload is a seminal unsigned essay
by Woolf on the front page of the *Times Literary
Supplement* published on Thursday 10 April 1919
and entitled 'Modern Novels'. In it, Woolf accuses
Bennett and others of her predecessors of 'materi-
alism' – of taking 'too much delight in the solidity
of [their] fabric' – comparing Bennett's novels 'to
well-built houses in which nobody lives'. Bennett,
for Woolf, is one of the worst culprits because he is
one of the best workmen, one 'who can make a book
so well constructed and solid in its craftsmanship
that . . . [t]here is not so much as a draught between
the frames of the windows, or a crack in the boards'.
Yet this 'magnificent apparatus for catching life' is
built 'just an inch or two on the wrong side' – such
that it, and other fiction then in vogue, missed, for
Woolf, the essential thing, whatever we call it: 'life or
spirit, truth or reality'.

It took Bennett nearly four years to respond. His
'Is the Novel Decaying?' (the title suggesting the
perennial supposed crisis of the form) of March
1923 argues that, while plot, style, invention, originality of outlook, 'wide information' and wide
sympathy are important, 'none of these counts

anything like so much as the convincingness of the characters.' These characters must then clash with each other as a means of producing strong emotion, something that is impossible with characters that are unconvincing: 'You cannot get strength out of falsity.' His charge against Woolf and others of the younger generation of novelists was that while displaying originality, ingenuity and style, they were too interested in detail to fully inhabit their characters. Citing Woolf's *Jacob's Room*, published the year before, 'as characteristic of the new novelists who have recently gained the attention of the alert and the curious', his conclusion is that its 'characters do not vitally survive in the mind, because the author has been obsessed by details of originality and cleverness'. Woolf disparaged this, two months later in her diary, as 'the old post-Dostoevsky argument' about the dissipation of character 'into shreds'. Yet, as Hynes indicates, by choosing characterisation as the key issue, 'Bennett had inadvertently chosen the battlefield for the quarrel that followed.'

Bennett and Woolf reiterated – and hardened – their critical positions in the summer of 1924 when they appeared together in 'What is a Good Novel?', a symposium published in *The Highway*. While Bennett argued, there, that good fiction depends on both character and plot, Woolf's position was that 'a good novel need not have a plot; need not have a happy ending; need not be about nice or respectable people; need not be in the least like life as we know it'. This is the first time, for Hynes, that their critical attitudes are 'orthogonal'; this is the moment, then, that they became self-conscious 'representatives of opposed schools'.

ı)) ▶ ▶ ▶

The course of my writing life was redirected a few months after returning from Barcelona by a woman for whom the 'black is beautiful' sobriquet could have been invented. A sixties icon – as actress, singer and model – Marsha Hunt established the Saga Prize for black British fiction in the mid-nineties at a time when black British novels hardly existed. An article in the *Observer* indicated that the first winner – Diran Adebayo for *Some Kind of Black* – would be receiving his prize on that day in mid-August at the Edinburgh Book Festival. Marsha, though, was keen to stress that the prize and that year's winner should be seen as 'separate subjects'; although delighted by the novel, this did not mean that 'hip metropolitan fiction' like Adebayo's was necessarily the order of the day. It would be great, she suggested, 'if next year a 95-year-old woman from Cromer [in Norfolk] were to win the prize'.

Having attended Marsha's Black and Asian writing retreat at the Arvon Foundation's Totleigh Barton centre in Sheepwash, Devon, that winter, I took her one-to-one advice to heart: that I should write a conventional novel before attempting to experiment. That I should travel so far down this extensive literary cul-de-sac was, perhaps, in retrospect, inevitable and unavoidable.

In his essay 'Modernism and Imperialism', the American theorist Fredric Jameson argues that since representation 'is governed by an "intention towards totality"' (a phrase he borrows from Lukács), the limits of the economic system must somehow be 'drawn back into the system [of the novel]' through being marked as an image. This he illustrates through a close reading of a passage from the opening pages of E. M. Forster's *Howards End*.

The train sped northward, under innumerable tunnels. It was only an hour's journey, but Mrs Munt had to raise and lower the window again and again. She passed through the South Welwyn

Tunnel, of tragic fame. She traversed the immense viaduct, whose arches span untroubled meadows and the dreamy flow of Tewin Water. She skirted the parks of politicians. At times the Great North Road accompanied her, more suggestive of infinity than any railway, awakening, after a nap of a hundred years, to such life as is conferred by the stench of motorcars, and to such culture as is implied by the advertisements of antibilious pills. To history, to tragedy, to the past, to the future, Mrs Munt remained equally indifferent; hers but to concentrate on the end of her journey, and to rescue poor Helen from this dreadful mess.

The word that stands out in this passage, for Jameson, is 'infinity'; this 'oddly disrupts' an otherwise conventional description of a train journey and seems to open up an unusual space outside the 'empirical' setting. What Jameson calls the 'metonymic contiguity' of the ancient highway and the modern railway – the substitution of their terms, one for the other, particularly as a means of representing the latter – is actually a means of 'disclosing some third reality' above and beyond the traditional or the modern. This other, 'vaster, unrepresentable space' stands in relation to the labelled empirical objects in the same way that the 'abstract word "infinity"' stands in relation to 'the conventional language in which it is embedded' – in the sense, however, of being some sort of afterthought or 'insignificant aside'.

It is, in a sense, London – the cosmopolitan centre – that is specifically the infinity that we catch a glimpse of along the Great North Road – or at least a 'caricature' of it (to use Forster's own word for it, as Jameson does). This invokes, for Jameson, a series of terms – antibilious pills and the stench of motorcars, cosmopolitanism and the nomadic – which, rather than representing modern urbanism or 'the faceless industrial masses of *The Waste Land*' bears, instead, another familiar name: that of the 'Empire, to give it its period designation'. It is, then, the imperial that contains the capacity to stretch the roads out to infinity, an infinity that is beyond the boundaries and the borders of the nation state. It is the imperial that is capable of leaving London behind as 'a new kind of spatial agglomeration or disease' whose commercialism 'throws up . . . practical and public beings' like Henry Wilcox, the owner (with his wife, Ruth) of the country house, 'the Howards End of the title', having amassed his wealth running the Imperial and West African Rubber Company.

Part of the imperial system thus manifests itself in human form – or, at least, in the narrative representation of that form that we call character. Yet this representation, for Jameson, is incomplete 'and thereby epistemologically distorted and misleading' in that it only shows the 'Imperial type' turned inwards, towards the metropolis. What is lacking, in short, is 'the other pole of the relationship' – the one, in fact, that essentially and fundamentally defines this type within its imperial function. After all, 'the persons of the colonised' are, and remain, 'structurally occluded' from this picture; they are beyond the apparent limits of the system. They are, however, drawn back into it via the representation of the Great North Road as an 'infinity', with the style of literary modernism represented by this 'new spatial language' becoming the substitute for, and marker of, this otherwise unrepresentable totality.

One way in which to test Jameson's hypothesis about an emerging 'style' within literary modernism and its relationship with how the imperial world system is (or isn't) represented is by way of what he calls a 'thought experiment'. Such a test or experiment would require an exceptional situation that somehow involves the simultaneous coexistence of the two otherwise incommensurable realities of colony and metropolis. It would presuppose, if it were possible, 'a national situation which reproduces the appearance of First World social reality and social relationships – perhaps through the coincidence of its language with the imperial language – but whose underlying structure is in fact much closer to that of [what would come to be called] the Third World or of colonised daily life'.

A literary modernism that emerges in such conditions could then be scrutinised as a means of differentiating it from works – such as *Howards End* – produced within the metropolis itself. Such a situation does, of course, exist – one that Jameson has had in mind all along: that of Ireland. And the novel he has also had in mind throughout is *Ulysses*.

It is in *Ulysses*, then, that this *a priori* deduction finds its 'immediate historical confirmation' in the sense that its setting – ostensibly, of course, Dublin during the course of Thursday 16 June 1904 – is, in fact, 'a radically different kind of space', one that is 'no longer central, as in English life', but is instead peripheral, marginal, 'ec-centric' like those of the colonised within the imperial system. It is, then, this 'colonised space' that radically transforms the project of literary modernism while 'retaining a distant family likeness to its imperial variants'. And it is by appropriating the spatial properties of the *Odyssey* – the one classical narrative whose enclosure encompasses an 'equally closed region of the globe' – that Joyce manages, through his extraordinary literary monument, to subvert and transcend the imperial relationship.

⊢ ⊱ ⊱ ⊱ ⊱ ⊱

The trend of modern fiction identified as problematic by Carruthers – 'from objective to subjective, from outer semblance to alleged inner reality' – deepened further in the interwar period before emerging after World War II into a fully fledged, more or less hermetically sealed box. This emergence was, in part, a response to the works of the modernists in the interwar period in terms of a further theorisation of what had been transpiring during that period; the 'belated product' of an ideology of modernism (as Jameson puts it in *A Singular Modernity*) formed the basis for novelists emerging from within this tradition in the wake of World War II. Indeed, for Jameson, it was the very 'invention' or 'innovation' of a more thoroughgoing theory of modernism in the years following World War II that enabled such writers to fashion novels in response to it, with 'Nabokov [being] unlike Joyce first and foremost by virtue of the fact

that Joyce already existed'. This type of imitation –
with the theory serving as a model – was unavailable
to what Jameson calls the 'classical' or 'high' modernists: Woolf, Joyce *et al*. They instead had to adopt
a particular approach to allegory – what T. S. Eliot,
in relation to *Ulysses*, famously called Joyce's mythic
method of appropriating the classical Homeric myth
of *The Odyssey* – to establish themselves in a world
that was devoid of their ideas.

The 'late modernists', then, had a more fully
formed theory with which to engage in their work –
a 'codification of the older modernist practices and
their organisation into a convention that serve[d]
as a model'. It was an ideology characterised, for
Jameson, by the concept of 'the autonomy of the
aesthetic': the idea, derived from the other arts,
of a preoccupation with the material and formal
equivalents 'of oil painting and the surface of the
canvas'. For Jameson, the classical moderns had
been self-conscious and reflexive in relation to
representation itself, allowing it 'to follow its own
semi-autonomous course, according to its own inner
logic', as in Woolf's famous injunction to 'record
the atoms as they fall upon the mind in the order
in which they fall'. Instead, the more or less fully
autonomous work of the late modernists achieved its

effects through the construction of a 'pure repetitive loop from which content is decisively excluded', an autonomy that was played out at the level of plot and style through what Jameson calls 'a closing of the circuit'. This sealing of the narrative was achieved, for instance, through character 'doubles' – Quilty, for instance, being 'a bad double' of Humbert Humbert in Nabokov's *Lolita* – or through the claustrophobic 'circularities' of the later plays and novels of Samuel Beckett.

Such circularities and characterological resonances are perhaps best characterised in relation to Bakhtin's concept of 'architectonics', which Michael Holquist describes, in his introduction to *Art and Answerability*, a collection of Bakhtin's early philosophical essays, as 'the general study of how entities relate to each other'. Concerning itself with building and with the way things are put together, Holquist stresses that the importance Bakhtin placed, within the concept, upon the interrelationship between subject and object, self and other, or author and protagonist, is not 'a mechanical concern for binary oppositions', but is, rather, a means of understanding the architectonics governing the relations between them. Nor is architectonics a matter of creating static structures; it is, instead, an *activity*, with the relations it describes always, for Holquist, being 'in a state of dynamic tension'. Wholes, then, for Bakhtin, are never given but must instead be achieved, with the work being the struggle towards the 'consummation' of constructing a whole 'out of the potential chaos of parts'.

Beckett's concern for architectonics is expressed from the outset of his writing career. His first novel, *Dream of Fair to Middling Women*, was written in 1932, as a twenty-six-year-old Beckett tried to free himself from the influence of Joyce. Part of the narrator's prior writerly aspiration is stated explicitly (although also somewhat dismissively) here as being 'once upon a time inclined to fancy ourself as the Cézanne, shall we say, of the printed page, very strong on architectonics'. This aspiration finds more implicit expression in Beckett's 'closed space' stories from the mid-1960s, whose settings are constructed from 'material of a strictly peculiar order, incommensurable with all human expressions whatsoever' (as Beckett wrote of the landscape in Cézanne's painting of *Mont Sainte-Victoire* in the Tate Gallery). Ostensibly concerned merely with the interaction between 'a body' and 'a place' (where in fact, as figments, there is neither), these short prose pieces are profound meditations on the nature of the creative imagination itself. Part of the conceit is in fact, at times, imagining the nature of a failure in the creative imagination, as in 'Imagination Dead Imagine'. Here, the fact that there is '[no] trace anywhere of life', that '[i]slands, waters, azure, verdure' after 'one glimpse' are omitted, vanishing endlessly – that the imagination itself is dead – presents 'no difficulty'. Instead of the interaction between conventional characters and settings we have two seemingly inanimate bodies 'bent in three', lying on their right sides such that they are 'back to back head to arse'. Each is located within its own semicircle on the ground of a rotunda three feet high and three wide that is 'all white in the [surrounding] whiteness'. This vault contains '[n]o way in' and none out, the only movement being that of each of the bodies' left eyes, 'which at incalculable intervals suddenly open wide and gaze in unblinking exposure long beyond what is humanly possible', as though trying to make sense of their shared predicament.

The expression of this minimalistic architectonics culminates in Beckett's late novel *Worstward Ho*, whose title derives partly from Edgar's speech in *King Lear* – 'O gods! Who is't can say "I am at the worst"?' – as well as from Charles Kingsley's 1855 novel, *Westward Ho!*. Beckett's concern, here, is with the failure of language to truly capture anything of experience and perception. As his biographer James Knowlson indicates, the language 'is deliberately pared down, reduced to a few lexical items assembled in a variety of combinations' with the intention of reaching towards 'an "unworsenable worse".'

> First the body. No. First the place. No. First both. Now either. Now the other. Sick of the either try the other. Sick of it back sick of the either. So on. Somehow on. Till sick of both. Throw up and go. Where neither. Till sick of there. Throw up and back. The body again. Where none. The place again. Where none. Try again. Fail again. Better again. Or better worse. Fail worse again. Still worse again. Till sick for good. Throw up for good. Go for good. Where neither for good. Good and all.

This, then, is the original purpose of the often quoted – and misappropriated – line from the same work: 'Try again. Fail again. Fail better.' It is the prior acknowledgement that in using words one cannot *but* fail, but that something of value may be communicated through that inevitable failure in the writing process.

This is arguably of a different order to how Deleuze and Guattari characterise the artistic

process: as the development of 'a plane of composition' that cuts through intersecting architectonic
frames, opening them to 'an infinite field of forces'
as a means of breathing life into the compound of
sensations. Beckett's approach in his late work is,
instead, more akin to that of science – a method
that, for Deleuze and Guattari, involves exploring
the functional interrelationship of variables 'that
have become independent by slowing down', which
is to say by eliminating any other variables (such as
the elements of so-called 'realistic' settings) that are
'liable to interfere' with the functions under investi-
gation. Beckett thus creates a cognitive laboratory
within which to isolate and investigate the nature of
the compositional process itself via an exploration
of the relationship between author and characters,
self and world, part and whole, a creative process
that is still, for now, reliant on the gaze of 'partial'
(rather than 'total') observers who are 'internal to
the domains under consideration'.

Yet the new 'aesthetic contingency' displayed in
this work is betrayed repeatedly, for Jameson, by the
refusal of an 'anecdotal core' to be assimilated. For
Jameson this inassimilable content is constitutive
of the late modernist work itself, as in 'the paradig-
matic nature of Beckett's late plays' (or equally, and

perhaps more emphatically, in the Nobel laureate's late novels). We have the shock of discovering, 'at the heart of these eternally recurring spectacles, an empirical situation – [an] unhappy marriage, intolerable youthful memories, a banal family structure, with irreducible names and characters . . .' – material that might, in other words, have been that of a 'dreary realist novel' but which instead persists, in the works of late modernism, as 'the indigestible brute facts to which the form reverts over and over again in its vain attempt to dissolve them'. The autonomous form and the inassimilable anecdotal content on which it depends are, then, for Jameson, 'in a necessary dialectical relation with each other and indeed produce each other reciprocally'. The work of the late modernists consists, on this basis, precisely in this dialectical process constituting 'the experience of the failure of autonomy to go all the way and fulfil its aesthetic programme'.

This, though, was 'a fortunate failure', according to Jameson, in that 'the replacement of the varied and incomprehensible Absolutes of modernism by the far more modest and comprehensible aesthetic autonomies of the late modern' enabled a much more accessible literature to be produced, a literature whose '"greatness" and timeless permanence' postmodernism, in turn, 'attempt[ed] radically to break'. It was fortunate, though, in a further – and much more important – sense, in that it provided the basis for a fuller and more thoroughgoing autonomy to emerge, one capable of paving the way out of its own impasse. The emerging architectonic is, then, one in which the novel truly begins to think itself into existence, and not just through the emergence of large language models and artificial intelligence but via its own enduring and inassimilable 'anecdotal core' of plot and character.

Nominal Verisimilitude: The Future of Plot and Character

Virginia Woolf's essay 'Character in Fiction' (published in *The Criterion* in 1924) is illustrated by a railway journey she took from Richmond to Waterloo. Late for the train, she boards the first carriage she comes to and immediately senses she has interrupted an uncomfortable conversation between an elderly woman (who she refers to as 'Mrs Brown') and a man ('Mr Smith') sitting opposite. Woolf proceeds to describe these 'characters' – their clothes, attitudes and sensibilities – and the supposed conflict between them, with the man, having been leaning over and talking emphatically to the woman, now sitting back and becoming silent, disturbed and annoyed by Woolf's presence. After an exchange of strained pleasantries, during which Mrs Brown has wiped away tears, the man resumes the topic at hand:

'So about that matter we were discussing. It'll be all right? George will be there on Tuesday?'

'We shan't be late,' said Mrs Brown, gathering herself together with superb dignity.

Smith disembarks before the train has fully stopped at Clapham Junction, and Woolf is left with the old woman sitting in the corner opposite making an almost overwhelming impression on her as she sits steeped in 'her atmosphere'.

Myriads of irrelevant and incongruous ideas crowd into one's head on such occasions; one sees the person, one sees Mrs Brown, in the centre of all sorts of different scenes. I thought of her in a sea-side house, among queer ornaments: sea-urchins, models of ships in glass cases. Her husband's medals were on the mantelpiece. She popped in and out of the room, perching on the edges of chairs, picking meals out of saucers, indulging in long, silent stares . . . And then, into this fantastic and secluded life, in broke Mr Smith. I saw him blowing in, so to speak, on a windy day. He banged, he slammed. His dripping umbrella made a pool in the hall. They sat closeted together.

Woolf's purpose in recounting the anecdote is to illustrate how a character imposes themselves on another person. Here, then, is 'Mrs Brown making someone begin almost automatically to write a novel about her'; all novels, for Woolf, begin 'with an old lady in the corner opposite'.

⏐ ⏐ ▸ ▸ ▸ ▸

The old lady in the corner opposite who helped initiate my first novel was a friend of my maternal grandmother's called Lynn who'd worked in the Women's Land Army during the war. They'd met when they were both being treated in hospital for rheumatoid arthritis, with Lynn – who my mother thought of as a difficult woman and as a bad influence on her mother – intermittently visiting us in the Norfolk village where we lived in the years following their discharge. My novel would also be inspired by the story a school friend of mine had told me about her grandmother handing over a World War II ration book at the checkout of the local supermarket whilst paying for her groceries and getting enraged when told she no longer needed it. Really, though, the book would be about my own family – my working-class white mother, my Nigerian father, and my maternal grandmother who,

with my grandfather, had not spoken to my parents
for six months after I was born in east London at the
end of the sixties.

Perhaps it was my first job after graduating – writing technical literature for an engineering company
in Denmark as part of an international team of
writers and translators – that led me to think that
the author should be an omniscient absence and
that characters could be transposed from real-life
encounters straightforwardly onto the page, with
this naïve re-presentation of reality associated in
my mind with 'the conventional novel'. Having left
a subsequent job in trying to finish it and spending
successive winters in Mexico writing and immersing
myself in the work and lives of Joyce and Beckett
in particular, my characters remained stubborn and
inert, their actions forced, their dialogue stilted. If, as
the novelist Hanif Kureishi has said, 'first novels are
letters to one's parents, telling them how it was for
you', then it's tempting to say that mine had somehow got lost in the post. In truth, though, the book
hadn't even got that far.

Bakhtin began theorising about authorial voice
in the novel around the time that Woolf was first

presenting her paper 'Mr Bennett and Mrs Brown' (which became 'Character in Fiction') to the Heretics Club, a society at Girton College, Cambridge. Central to his thesis on Dostoevsky, eventually published in 1929 as *Problems of Dostoevsky's Art*, is the novelist's 'revolutionary innovation in the field of the novel as an artistic form', which Bakhtin called 'dialogism' (just as the fundamental unit of his colleague Valentin Vološinov's philosophy of language is not the word or sentence but 'the interaction of at least two utterances – in a word, dialogue'). Dialogism refers, then, to a situation in which two 'voices', that of the author and that of the character – what Bakhtin calls 'dual directedness' – are present in a single line of discourse.

The idea – which is of central importance to a conception of the novel in the present and the future – received perhaps its fullest expression in Bakhtin's *Discourse in the Novel*. Bakhtin had been making plans to broaden and elaborate on his study of Dostoevsky almost as soon as it was published. In his subsequent long essay, the dual has become multiple, the writer faced with an internally fragmented linguistic world, fractured by differences in form, voice and habit. It is a world Bakhtin calls 'heteroglossia' (literally 'varied-speechedness'), the name he gave to the 'inner stratification of a single national language into social dialects, group mannerisms, professional jargons, generic languages, the languages of generations and age-groups' and so on, with this inner stratification 'at every given moment of its historical existence [being] a necessary prerequisite for the genre of the novel'. The novel, in other words, uses social heteroglossia and individual multivoicedness to orchestrate its themes as a means of representing and expressing 'the whole objective, meaningful world'. The novelist 'always and everywhere (in all the historic literary epochs known to us) finds "languages" rather than language, [with the active literary consciousness] confronted by the necessity of *having to choose a language*'.

According to Bakhtin scholar Ken Hirschkop, there was 'not the slightest need for metaphor' for postcolonial theorists of the novel: dialogism was perfectly ordinary for the descendants and diasporas of former colonies. Questions around which language to use – which, for Bakhtin, meant how 'centripetal' Latin related to the emerging 'centrifugal' European vernaculars – have found profound contemporary echoes and resonances in our era. W. E. B. Du Bois' famous claim, for instance, that black Americans 'were afflicted with a "double consciousness, this sense of always looking at oneself through the eyes of others", uncannily mirrored Bakhtin's notion [in *Problems of Dostoevsky's Art*] of a discourse directed "both at the referent of the speech, as in ordinary discourse, and at *the discourse of an other*, at *someone else's speech*"'.

Henry Louis Gates Jr., in particular, 'makes good' on Bakhtin's claim that the double-voicedness that is typical of the novel derives its breadth and vivacity from popular genres. Just as for Bakhtin, where the techniques for constructing novelistic language were devised 'on a local scale, in the minor "low" genres, on the popular stages, in the fairground squares, in street songs and anecdotes', so (according to Gates) with black vernacular traditions, with their centuries-old tradition of 'signifying'. Such signifying extends beyond the Standard English usage into the African-American community where 'it is possible to say "He is signifying" and "Stop signifying"' (according to anthropologist Claudia Mitchell-Kernan), with this vernacular usage, as Hirschkop says, appropriated 'into African American literary techniques'.

There are further resonances with Bakhtin, who speaks of the 'three prominent types' within the 'low folkloric and semifolkloric' forms of literature from the Middle Ages – the rogue, the clown and the fool. These figures are 'enormously significant for the later development of the European novel', in part through acting as intermediaries between high and low culture, as Bakhtin explored in his seminal book about Rabelais' novels. Their equivalent within the African-American tradition, according to Gates, is 'of the order of the trickster figure of Yoruba mythology (*Esu-Elegbara* in Nigeria and *Legba* among the *Fon* in Dahomey)', with these trickster figures also primarily serving as mediators between the high and the low, between the people and the gods: *Èṣù Elegbára* (to give him his diacritic dues), for instance, is the master of the interface between the profane and the divine.

Yet Hirschkop also argues that Bakhtin's project was not to recognise the multiplicity of voices encountered in the social world (which in my case primarily meant my diverse domestic environment) – to 'corral and organise' an existing dialogism – but to represent language artistically through stylising, parodying or ironising it. Returning from a further three-month winter writing retreat in Latin America – this time primarily in the foothills of the Andes in Chile – I was, perhaps, starting to understand this. Then my father died, and everything changed.

▸ ▸ ▸ ▸ ▸ ▸

The first result of the 'awakening' of English-speaking writers to Dostoevsky (as the first translations appeared during the second decade of the twentieth century) was, for Carruthers, 'oddly perverse' in that his greatness as a novelist – his extraordinary insight into human nature, his intense dramatic effects, his mastery of dialogue, the power with which he integrated diverse and often contradictory aspects of character into figures as unique as Tolstoy's – was largely overlooked. Instead he was primarily addressed as 'a great thinker', with his ideas pored over and debated by his followers. To the extent that his practice as a novelist was considered, it was assumed to have resulted in possibly the final defeat of form, whereas he had, in fact, 'a much stronger sense of plot than Tolstoy.' The latter, for Carruthers, was more formless and analytical than the 'intensely dramatic' Dostoevsky, yet it was formlessness that became fashionable, and it was this, primarily, that dealt a decisive blow to plot.

Carruthers may have been responding in this (as Bennett did) to the provocations of Woolf's 'Modern Novels' essay. In it, Woolf asserts that 'if one were free and could set down what one chose, there would be no plot, little probability, and a vague general confusion in which the clear-cut features of the tragic, the comic, the passionate, and the lyrical were dissolved beyond the possibility of separate recognition'. She continues:

> The mind, exposed to the ordinary course of life, receives upon its surface a myriad impressions – trivial, fantastic, evanescent, or engraved with the sharpness of steel. From all sides they come, an incessant shower of innumerable atoms, composing in their sum what we might venture to call life itself; and to figure further as the semi-transparent envelope, or luminous halo, surrounding us from the beginning of consciousness to the end. Is it not perhaps the chief task of the novelist to convey this incessantly varying spirit with whatever stress or sudden deviation it may display, and as little admixture of the alien and external as possible? We are not pleading merely for courage and sincerity; but suggesting that the proper stuff for fiction is a little other than custom would have us believe it.

Woolf, then, was concerned with revealing 'the innermost flame which flashes its myriad messages through the brain', with recording 'the atoms as they fall upon the mind in the order they fall': in tracing the pattern, however disconnected or incoherent it appears, 'which each sight or incident scores upon the consciousness'. Rather than with what she takes to be 'adventitious' – something not inherent to the novel as a form, suggesting dismissively that plot is one of 'the handrails to which we cling for support when we set our imagination free' – it is something to be disregard or discarded 'with complete courage'.

Woolf's views also reverberate through Forster's prevarications on plot and story (in *Aspects of the Novel*), which he distinguishes, ingeniously although somewhat simplistically, with the following well-known example: '"The king died and then the queen died" is a story. "The king died and then the queen died of grief" is a plot.' In answer to the question of what a novel does, comes the regretful, somewhat sad reply of 'oh dear yes – the novel tells a story'. The basis of a novel is, then, however regrettably, a story, something Forster defines straightforwardly as 'a narrative of events arranged in a time-sequence'. The question then becomes whether the novelist can 'abolish' such 'base and inferior' sequences from their work while still referring to that work as a novel.

There was, for Forster, one novelist who had attempted this. Gertrude Stein had gone 'much further [even] than Emily Brontë, Sterne or Proust' in her attempt at the abolishment of time. Indeed she had 'smashed up and pulverised her clock', scattering its fragments around the world 'like the limbs of [the Egyptian god] Osiris', albeit with the noble purpose of hoping to free fiction from time's 'tyranny' to enable it to express, more fully and truthfully, a life of value. Although there was nothing, for Forster, to ridicule in her experiment (hence his expression of regret), Stein fails, for him, because fiction that is devoid of time is incapable of expression. In other words, the time-sequence cannot be abolished without carrying with it – to ruin – 'all that should have taken its place', such as the 'radiant alternative' of expressing values alone.

Forster seems more amenable, however, to the abolishment of plot. This he defines as a time-sequence with an emphasis on 'causality': the time-sequence of the monarchs' demise is retained, but it is over-shadowed by the 'sense of causality', the death arising *because* of the pre-decease. Forster's question in relation to plot is whether it provides the best possible framework for a novel.

> After all, why has a novel to be planned? Cannot it grow? Why need it close, as a play closes? Cannot it open out? Instead of standing above his work and controlling it, cannot the novelist throw himself

into it and be carried along to some goal that he does not foresee? The plot is exciting and may be beautiful, yet is it not a fetish, borrowed from the drama, from the spatial limitations of the stage? Cannot fiction devise a framework that is not so logical yet more suitable to its genius?

Forster's examination of this potential abolishment is illustrated in relation to a novel, published two years previously, that had provided 'a violent assault' on plot (as Forster defined it) as well as 'a constructive attempt' at putting something else in its place.

André Gide's *Les Faux-Monnayeurs* (*The Counterfeiters*) does contain a plot of 'the logical objective' sort identified by Forster – or, rather, 'fragments of plots'; these constitute 'a successful creation' along familiar lines. They are not, however, the centrepiece of the book; that which lies nearest to the centre, for Forster, is 'a discussion about the art of the novel' which takes place between Edouard, a novelist, Bernard, his secretary, and some of their friends. Edouard has been exploring what Forster calls 'the old thesis' (from Plato) of truth in life not being the same as truth in art, and has stated that he aspires to write a novel that includes both truth-types.

'And what is its subject?' asked Sophroniska.

'There is none,' said Edouard sharply. 'My novel has no subject. No doubt that sounds foolish. Let us say, if you prefer, that it will not have "a" subject. . . . "A slice of life," the naturalistic school used to say. The mistake that school made was always to cut its slice in the same direction, always lengthwise, in the direction of time. Why not cut it up and down? Or across? As for me, I don't want to cut it at all. You see what I mean. I want to put everything into my novel and not snip off my material either here or there. I have been working for a year, and there is nothing I haven't put in: all I see, all I know, all I can learn from other people's lives and my own.'

'My poor man, you will bore your readers to death,' cried Laura, unable to restrain her mirth.

'Not at all. To get my effect, I am inventing, as my central character, a novelist, and the subject of my book will be the struggle between what reality offers him and what he tries to make of the offer.'

'Have you planned out this book?' asked Sophroniska, trying to keep grave.

'Of course not.'

'Why "of course"?'

'For a book of this type any plan would be unsuitable. The whole of it would go wrong if I decided any detail ahead. I am waiting for reality to dictate to me.'

'But I thought you wanted to get away from reality.'

'My novelist wants to get away, but I keep pulling him back. To tell the truth, this is my subject: the struggle between facts as proposed by reality, and the ideal reality.'

'Do tell us the name of this book,' said Laura, in despair.

'Very well. Tell it them, Bernard.'

'*Les Faux Monnayeurs*,' said Bernard. 'And now will you please tell us who these faux monnayeurs are.'

'I haven't the least idea.'

Bernard and Laura looked at each other and then at Sophroniska. There was the sound of a deep sigh.

This is a translation and paraphrase, by Forster, of the passage he considers to be the centrepiece of the novel, a passage that continues with the arrival of the 'false coin' of the title. The reason for its importance lies in its attempt at combining 'the two truths' (represented by truth and falsity in the currency) and in the aspirations of the novelist to be 'carried

away' by the material of the novel – to let themselves be 'rolled over and over by it' – rather than
being 'subdued' by it; ideas about forgery, inflation
and depreciation had, after all, 'gradually invaded'
Edouard's book (just as theories of clothing invade
Thomas Carlyle's novel *Sartor Resartus*) to the
point of assuming 'the functions of characters'. The
purpose, in other words, is to stand up to the twin
tyrannies of plot and character, while adopting their
'clothing' during the course of the novel.

Forster concludes, however, without providing
any further instructions on how to achieve this: it is
Bakhtin who – as so often – must step in to assist.
His *Problems of Dostoevsky's Art* contains the key
to opening up the place of plot in the future of the
form. In what he describes as the 'monological'
novels of the past, protagonists are 'generated by
the plot itself' (in the sense of being formed and
re-formed in the adversity inherent in the plot's
turning points). In contrast, the plot in the 'polyphonic' novel – the novel of the future – though
still, crucially, present, fulfils a distinctly subsidiary
function: that of merely supplying the 'clothing that
dresses' the protagonist. Forster hints at this even-
tuality, by stating quite straightforwardly that the
'lowest and simplest of literary organisms' – the

story – really only has 'one merit': that of inducing a reader, through whatever means, to turn the page. This may be done via the traditional Aristotelian narrative arc – a wave – or via other narrative patterns and designs (such as those explored in Jane Alison's *Meander, Spiral, Explode*: the radials of Gabriel García Márquez's *Chronicle of a Death Foretold* or Alain Robbe-Grillet's *Jealousy*, the networks and cells of W. G. Sebald's *The Emigrants*, or the fractals of Clarence Lispector's 'The Fifth Story' or Anne Carson's *Nox*, to name just a few). Woolf is right, then, to speak of plot as a handrail, but not in stating that this adventitious support is superfluous or unnecessary and should be discarded. After all, without some such page-turning mechanism – whether 'causal' or otherwise – the novel can hardly be said to have a future.

᠂ ᠂ ᠂ ▶ ▶ ▶

Kerouac's technique of 'sketching' scenes and people from life worked well for him (according to his biographer Gerald Nicosia), in that it allowed him to make the writing process itself the subject of the writing. He had been intrigued for years, not so much by *what* he was describing, as by *how* and *why* he was describing it.

A contemporary way of saying this is, of course, that Jack was writing autofiction (before autofiction was a thing). This form shares something with the German *Künstlerroman*, a book that, in describing the maturation of an artist, foregrounds the status of the narrator, protagonist or authorial alter ego as an artist or writer, and inscribes the book's creation within the book itself. To Christian Lorentzen's 2018 list of 'novels by the likes of Sheila Heti, Ben Lerner, Teju Cole, Jenny Offill and Tao Lin' – as well as the inevitable Karl Ove Knausgaard – could be added more recent works by Claire-Louise Bennett, Rachel Cusk, Eimear McBride, Jon Fosse and many others. What these works signify for Jonathon Sturgeon, another critic, is the death of the postmodern project of Thomas Pynchon, J. G. Ballard and Don DeLillo – a project in which late modernism is replaced by 'an ocean of hyperreality or unreality' (in the case of Ballard), or 'a system of disinformation, paranoia and entropy' (in the case of Pynchon and DeLillo) – in favour of a new future for the novel 'wherein the self is considered a living thing composed of fictions'. What's at stake is no longer the tired question about what constitutes the real as distinct from the fictional; instead these novels redistribute the relation between fiction and the self, treating literature (in the words of

Kenneth Burke's *The Philosophy of Literary Form*)
as 'equipment for living'. In doing so, they foreclose,
for Sturgeon, 'the exhausted conversation' about the
nature of 'realism', replacing it with a literature that
is 'a living hypothesis' exploring questions of how a
person should be (to paraphrase the title of one of
Sheila Heti's autofictions) – and, more specifically,
exploring the process of creating fiction itself.

This finds further expression in the contemporary
period through what Timothy Bewes in *Free Indirect:
The Novel in a Postfictional Age* calls 'the breakdown in the instantiation relation' – a breakdown
which, 'on a certain reading of contemporary fiction'
can be described as the twenty-first-century novel's
'overriding obsession'. Bewes illustrates this 'non-
instantiability' with reference to the opening of J.
M. Coetzee's 2003 novel *Elizabeth Costello*, which
establishes the disconnection between art and the
world as the condition of its own existence:

> There is first of all the problem of the opening,
> namely, how to get us from where we are, which
> is, as yet, nowhere, to the far bank. It is a simple
> bridging problem, a problem of knocking together
> a bridge. People solve such problems every day.
> They solve them, and having solved them push on.

Let us assume that, however it may have been done, it is done. Let us take it that the bridge is built and crossed, that we can put it out of our mind. We have left behind the territory in which we were. We are in the far territory, where we want to be.

Instead of joining 'the two territories' together – 'the world', with its 'logic of communicability', lying on one bank and 'the world of fiction, the novel' on the other – Coetzee's 'conceit' is to construct a bridge that actually 'ensures and maintains their separation'. Crossing the bridge would imply a communicability between these two worlds, a connection between what occurs within, and outside of, the work. The bridge is not crossed, though, in *Elizabeth Costello* – its crossing, at least, goes unnarrated. Instead 'the bridge must be "assume[d]" to be "built and crossed," and then "put . . . out of our mind[s]."'

Bewes defines instantiation as perhaps nothing more than this link – or bridge – between the world and the work. It is 'a form of connection that remains intact', for some literary critics, such as Dorothy J. Hale, who introduced the term, 'in the face of the many challenges to representation in the modern period'. Bewes argues that instantiation's 'economy of perception and expression' implies an author whose point-of-view is 'necessarily limited by its "social positionality"' (another term taken from Hale – in an essay on Zadie Smith's novel *On Beauty*). 'What is never quite entertained by Hale', for Bewes, is that the novel in question 'does not sustain any consistent perspective' (and this despite Smith's commentary on her own work); that it is not, in fact, a 'work of the transition from represen-tation to instantiation' but is, instead, like *Elizabeth Costello*, a work of what Bewes calls 'postfiction' – a work, that is, in which 'the instantiation relation is no longer supportable, in which point of view itself is abandoned'.

This represents, for Bewes, a new 'mode of thought [that has become] blazingly evident in English-language fiction' since *Elizabeth Costello* was published in 2003. It is not, for Bewes, that *Elizabeth Costello* inaugurates this mode – one that has, in fact, been present throughout the history of the novel – nor does it bear any responsibility for it; rather, 'Coetzee's novel is simply one of the works from our own period that illustrates it most clearly.'

❙ ❱ ❱ ❱ ❱ ❱

In his book *Beckett and the Cognitive Method*, narrative theorist Marco Bernini draws on contemporary
cognitive research to argue that voices in Beckett's
novels can be read as natural and non-pathological
expressions of 'inner speech' – the activity of talking
to and with oneself, within oneself – although an
inner speech that is 'detuned' or defamiliarised as a
means, in part, of exploring its functioning. Building
on recent cognitive models asserting that inner
speech is internalised public language rooted in social
interactions, which serves a developmental function in
(and beyond) childhood, Bernini argues that what is
internalised is 'not just a conversational grammar' but
(after Bakhtin) 'a "dialogic" intersubjective structure
that will shape the inner experience of "the dialogic
mind".' In other words, through interactions with care-
givers and the wider world, a child internalises multiple
(and sometimes conflicting) perspectives – as well as
the process and functioning of perspective-taking
itself – with inner speech representing the structure
and content of these perspectives on reality 'just as
the voices in external dialogue represent differing perspectives on the world'.

Bernini argues for the potential momentary revers-
ibility of this developmental process in adulthood
(such that the transition from external discourse to

'condensed' inner speech is switched), a process somehow accessed by Beckett and exploited by him from
Dream of Fair to Middling Women, his first novel
(written in 1932), onwards. The porosity and polar-
isation between inner and outer worlds, between the
introspective and the social, between self and other, is
one of *Dream*'s key themes, with its narrator speaking
of the 'fuss that went on about the monologue and
dialogue and polylogue and catalogue, all exclusively
intérieur'. Here the language is hardly metaphorical;
rather than a record of the speech of external 'actors',
then, this multivoicedness is an internalised social
experience, albeit one that is ultimately unlocatable.

   Yet at this stage in his career, Beckett still 'leaves
the polyphonic black box of the mind unopened',
according to Bernini. Its exploration is limited to
'heterophenomenology': Daniel Dennett's word
for the study of consciousness 'from the outside'.
It is only with the 'vision' in his mother's room
in Foxrock, County Dublin, in the aftermath of
World War II that Beckett liberates himself from
the influence of James Joyce, his friend and mentor,
and enters the territory of the mind more fully. This
profound moment is fictionalised in a relocated
position – the pier at Dún Laoghaire in Dublin –
and immortalised in his play *Krapp's Last Tape*:

'Spiritually a year of profound gloom and indigence until that memorable night in March, at the end of the jetty, in the howling wind, never to be forgotten, when suddenly I saw the whole thing. The vision at last . . .' Beckett's revelation marked a decisive commitment (according to James Knowlson) to 'his own inner world for his subjects'; he would use his imagination to filter and refract external reality, with inner drives and desires given greater freedom of expression; rational contradictions would be permitted, and the imagination would be allowed to formulate unconventional alternative worlds.

The moment in his mother's room also marked, then, a rejection of an approach to writing perfected by Joyce in which 'knowing more was a way of creatively understanding the world and controlling it'. Contrary to Carruthers' view in his essay on the future of the novel about its exteriorising direction of travel, it is through this progressive (and then decisive) abandonment (or inward incorporation) of outer reality that a trajectory for the future of the novel was inaugurated.

᾿ ﹜ ﹜ ▸ ▸ ▸

A few months after my father's death, we renewed my mother's passport – which had expired before my older brother was born – so that we could travel to Denmark, which my parents hadn't been able to visit when I was living there. Back then I'd been fortunate enough to rent a room in an elegant Copenhagen flat close to the waterfront on Sankt Annæ Plads from a kindly Danish couple; now, at a loose end and seeing the street name in a listings magazine during our stay, I suggested to my mum that we attend a concert there – of Bach cantatas performed by the Monteverdi Choir and the English Baroque Soloists in Garnisonskirken, a church a few doors down from where I'd lived but within which I had never set foot. My self-education in classical music had developed significantly since the days of exchanging my jazz CDs for the Danish couple's operas while I lived in their flat, yet nothing could have prepared me for what transpired in that hallowed hall that evening: a vision of infinite possibilities somehow glimpsed in – and through – the music.

A century on from Woolf, Carruthers and Bakhtin, and it is unremarkable for Rachel Cusk, one of our leading novelists, to say she is not interested in character because she thinks it no longer exists. In an interview with *New Yorker* critic Alexandra

Schwartz she speaks of driving over Brooklyn Bridge and recalling things she'd read about the infrastructure of American roads and bridges being in a state of disrepair, and making an analogy with the structures not just of the novel but of consciousness itself, which is also 'actually resting on old, possibly decrepit structures'. The conventional structure of the literary sentence came, for Cusk, to seem a lot like driving down Fifth Avenue, unthinkingly moving back and forth along well-established routes with their unexamined underpinning just because that is what had always been done. In her *Transit* trilogy and subsequent novels, Cusk avoids or undermines these conventional structures having identified some of the elements that underpin them. And character is one of those elements that has changed from the old templates: character, for Cusk, is no longer how living is being done.

Bewes' analysis of such trends in the contemporary novel hinges on liberating the term 'free indirect' from its traditional literary usage. Free indirect discourse is ordinarily described as a technique for representing a character's thought or speech that avoids both the quoted utterances of direct discourse ('"We shan't be late," said Mrs Brown') and the conventional framing syntax of indirect speech ('Mrs Brown said they wouldn't be late') in favour of a more immediate access to character. Bewes takes the first sentence of James Joyce's story 'The Dead' as a now well-known example cited by Bakhtin's colleague Vološinov: 'Lily, the caretaker's daughter, was literally run off her feet.' The narrator, whilst maintaining his independent position, is identified with his character through the simultaneous retention of Lily's word 'literally' (in preference to the more accurate 'figuratively', say, or 'metaphorically') and the omission of the reporting verb 'she thought'.

Contemporary creative and critical writing books tend to describe this as a 'merging', 'aligning' or 'intertwining' of viewpoints: a 'technique', according to Andrew Cowan in *The Art of Writing Fiction*, 'by which an author is able to achieve some of the immediacy and personality of first person narration while maintaining the authority and flexibility of the third person'. This closing of the gap – the 'psychic distance' – between 'the external voice of the narrator and the internal world of the character' enables the narrative to 'bend itself around that character' (for James Wood, in *How Fiction Works*), the narrative seeming to want to merge with the character, to adopt their mode of speaking or thinking through a kind of 'secret sharing'.

Another way in which free indirect discourse has been described is as a 'concealed', 'masked' or 'veiled' discourse – a characterisation Vološinov attributes to the linguist Theodor Kalepky. The form here, stylistically, takes on the characteristics of a puzzle, the point being to try to guess the identity of the 'speaker', since, for Vološinov, from a perspective of abstract grammar it is the author who speaks; from the perspective of the wider narrative context, it is the character who speaks. While Kalepky's analysis, according to Vološinov, represents a step forward from the idea of free indirect discourse as a merging of viewpoints, the analysis falls short of an adequate definition of what is transpiring. The main problem of Kalepky's approach, for Vološinov, is 'his interpreting a linguistic phenomenon within the framework of the *individual consciousness*'.

Rather than framing the contradictory aspects of free indirect discourse in relation to existing novelistic distinctions, then, such as those between author, narrator and character(s) (in other words, as a 'masked' or 'veiled' discourse, or as a modifica-tion or mixture of pre-existing forms of discourse), what was slowly and painstakingly being under-stood here – and theorised with clarity by Bakhtin and Vološinov for the first time – was a feature of the novel that many critics have since asserted to be nothing less than its 'unique discovery and invention' (in the words of Bewes): the dual (or even multiple) directedness of its language.

One of the consequences, for contemporary fiction and for the future of the novel, of what Bakhtin calls a 'revolutionary innovation in the field of the novel as an artistic form' is what Bewes identifies as the difficulty – perhaps the impossibility – of locating 'a point of nonfictional, anchored subjectivity from which an interpretation may take place that does not itself require, invite, further interpretation'. While acknowledging the risk of this infinite regress as 'a logic of perpetual interpretability', Bewes illustrates its application with reference to the following passage from *Elizabeth Costello*, which is interpolated by an unspecified character who may (or may not) be Elizabeth's son John:

Realism has never been comfortable with ideas. It could not be otherwise: realism is premised on the idea that ideas have no autonomous existence, can exist only in things. So when it needs to debate ideas, as here, realism is driven to invent situations – walks in the countryside, conversations – in which characters give voice to contending ideas and thereby in a certain sense embody them. The notion of *embodying* turns out to be pivotal. In such debates ideas do not and indeed cannot float free: they are tied to the speakers by whom they are enounced, and generated from the matrix of individual interests out of which their speakers act in the world – for instance, the son's concern that his mother not be treated as a Mickey Mouse post-colonial writer . . .

The passage cannot, for Bewes, be 'the reflection of a character in a narrative situation', since it is not presented as 'an animating idea of the work at all and asks nothing of us'; nor can it be the intervention of 'a disembodied narrator', since this 'disproves itself from the other side of the equation'. The idea expressed is, in short, incompatible with its own instantiation. It is 'like a pure utterance dropped into the text', a comment on the implications of the novel's opening paragraph delivered as if the bridge remained to be crossed, a place from which the statement's credibility and verifiability 'is still adjudicable.'

The truth, though, for Bewes, is that there is no 'ambiguity of focalisation' in Coetzee's passage since what is transpiring 'is not the presentation of an idea but the staging of an impossibility'. Instead, then, of a 'rhetoric of fiction' that presupposes 'an ultimate point of view (a consciousness) anchored within each work', what *Elizabeth Costello* gives expression to is the possibility of a perspective 'no longer saddled by affiliation', a 'deauthorisation' of literary discourse that Bewes labels the 'free indirect'. The 'free indirect', then – understood not as a 'style' or 'discourse' – is a non-anchored and non-centred perspective that relinquishes any claim to represent the perspectives of characters, narrators or authors. In other words, it is the way in which the 'technology' or literary apparatus of the novel itself is bringing into being its own thought or point-of-view, and one that cannot be inhabited subjectively precisely because it is not the thought of a character, author, narrator, or even a reader.

Bakhtin envisaged this innovation in the form – this future for the novel – through his concept of 'polyphony'. In a further development of his theory of dialogism, he proposed that a protagonist is similarly ambivalently involved in the action but in a new reweighted arrangement, and one in which the literary work (or author's perspective) no longer dominates them. This equalisation of perspectives between author and protagonist implies that the latter can address not only other characters

but also readers of the work – and in a much less
self-conscious and more genuine way than in postmodernism's phase of 'metafiction' (its preoccupation
with its own fictionality). According to Hirschkop,
the musical analogy was intended to indicate how
Dostoevsky created a novelistic form that was 'able
to resist authorial unification' (a state that Bakhtin,
using Balzac as an example, called 'systematically
monologic') as well as being able to avoid representing characters as objectified consciousnesses, closed
off and impermeable to each other.

The future of the novel lies, on this basis, in a
further foregrounding of the mechanisms by which
characters as 'autonomous subjects, not objects'
coexist and interact. It lies in the progressive abandonment of the conceit of the conventional, increasingly
exposing the workings and the acting out of unre-
solved internal conflicts between autonomous and
unfinalised consciousnesses – even to the extent of
relinquishing realistic character names and settings,
as the Norwegian author Jon Fosse has done in his
seminal seven-novel sequence *Septology*. Here, cap-
italised common names (The Clinic, The Country
Inn, The Lane, The Wharf . . .) confer a generality
(according to Blake Morrison in the *London Review
of Books*) 'as though we could be anywhere and with

anyone'. This nominal verisimilitude also extends to Fosse's characters: his two protagonists have the same name (Asle), and one of them is even married to someone whose name shares the same letters (Ales), these conceptual personae in their settings being the apparatus with which Fosse fashions what he calls 'mystical realism' but which might simply be called reality. It lies in the appropriation, from more popular storytelling forms, of off-the-peg non-formative plots, whether causal or otherwise, whose sole purpose is to induce us to turn the pages. Perhaps most importantly, the future of the novel lies in understanding more deeply how the world of the fictional character relates to the so-called real world, the world of the old lady in the corner opposite who supposedly makes someone begin almost automatically to write a novel about her.

Autopoietic Agents: The Future of the Novelist

On hearing that Jon Fosse had won the 2023 Nobel Prize in Literature, his English-language fiction publisher, Jacques Testard, described him as 'an exceptional writer, who has managed to find a totally unique way of writing fiction'. Testard refers to Fosse's Norwegian editor Cecilie Seiness as saying that 'if you open any book by Jon and read a couple of lines, it couldn't be written by anyone else.' This brings to mind Zadie Smith's view that 'an author's literary style is about conveying "the only possible expression of a particular human consciousness"' (in her 2007 essay 'Fail Better', quoted in Vauhini Vara's 'Confessions of a Viral AI Writer', for *Wired*). The repetition of the word 'consciousness' in Smith's essay reminds Vara of 'the debate among scientists and philosophers about whether AI is, or will ever be, conscious'. While falling 'well outside' her area of expertise, Vara does know what consciousness means to a writer: for her, as for Zadie, 'writing is an attempt to clarify what the world is like from where I stand in it.'

Perspective is one of a myriad of concerns triggered by the rise of generative AI and large language models. The writer, programmer and tech consultant Alex Reisner concluded a 2023 piece for *The Atlantic* with the sentiment that when algorithms are used to organise and filter human knowledge, 'the problem of perspective becomes both crucial and intractable'. Reisner's ingenuity and expertise had enabled him to access a hitherto secret database used to 'train' the models. A lawsuit filed by the authors Sarah Silverman, Richard Kadrey and Christopher Golden in California the previous month had alleged that Meta had used their books, in violation of copyright laws, to train LLaMa, its set of large language models. As the court filing indicates, a LLM is 'an AI software programme designed to emit convincingly naturalistic text outputs in response to user prompts'. Yet neither the filing nor the furore surrounding it had offered, for Reisner, 'a look under the hood': there had been no way of telling whether these or any other authors' books had been used to train LLaMa. In fact, the 'Books3' dataset – which contains in excess of 170,000 books, including fiction by Fosse and Zadie Smith as well as works by Silverman, Kadrey and Golden – had been used to train it and other generative AI programmes 'now embedded in websites across the internet'.

One of the most troubling aspects of generative AI, for Reisner, is that it is being developed in secret. Systems such as ChatGPT require vast amounts of written material to enable plausible, 'human-like' outputs, yet 'few people outside of companies such as Meta and OpenAI know the full extent of the texts these programmes have been trained on'. Earlier in the summer, Reisner had begun reading 'online discussions among academic and hobbyist AI developers' in an attempt to understand what types of books were being used to train the systems. This eventually led him to download 'a massive cache of training text' known as 'the Pile', which included the Books3 dataset. He then wrote a series of computer programmes to search the otherwise unmanageable Pile, initially for lines labelled 'Books3' and then for ISBNs, which he extracted and fed into another programmes connected to an online book data-base. This enabled him to retrieve author, title and publishing information which was then viewable in a spreadsheet. Reisner published this information as a searchable database on *The Atlantic*'s website ten days before the award of Fosse's Nobel Prize. The database includes around 57,000 works of fiction.

The US Authors Guild responded two days after the database was published. It thanked Reisner for breaking the 'incredibly important' story and acknowledged the unsettling nature of the revelations for authors around the world. It advised authors whose books are in the dataset to write to the AI companies concerned 'telling them that they do not have the right to use your books', and to sign an open letter to the companies' CEOs demanding they request permission and provide compensation for the use of the books. It also advised that authors take steps to prevent future unauthorised use, such as including a short 'no AI training' notice in their books, and blocking OpenAI's web crawler from accessing material published online. The guild had filed its own AI-related class-action lawsuit (against OpenAI) in New York City a week previously.

It is understandable, within this context, that technology – the most obvious prognostic category for the future of the novel – gets a bad name with many literary novelists. Yet most attack its continuing

emergence without acknowledging that the novel –
and writing – are themselves forms of technology.
Walter Ong's seminal *Orality and Literacy*
argues that the artificiality of writing has become
internalised to the point of seeming natural. More
than any other artificial creation, though, writing
is 'utterly invaluable and indeed essential for the
realisation of fuller, interior, human potentials', the
technology of writing capable, for Ong, of effecting
'interior transformations of consciousness'. The way
in which it does so is not through straightforwardly
expressing 'pregiven mental contents' (as narrative theorist Marco Bernini puts it), with ideas
pre-existing, and independent of, the act of writing. Aesthetic ideas emerge, instead, through – and
within – the coupled, continuously reciprocal two-
way device–mind process that we call fiction-writing,
with 'device' here encompassing the writer's material
tools of laptop or notebook as well as the intangi-
bles of character, plot, setting and point of view.
The trajectory of the novel has, then, been one of
continual extension – and re-purposing – of literary
apparatus, as exemplified in the stylistic encyclopedia that is *Ulysses*, in what Carruthers somewhat
dismissively calls Virginia Woolf's 'embroideries on
the commonplace', in the metafictional assaults of

the postmodernists, and continuing through Christian Lorentzen's categories of 'autobiographical fiction, autobiographical metafiction, and autofiction'.

The question then shifts from 'Will technology transform the novel of the future?' to 'In what new ways will this occur?'

⦙ ⦚ ▸ ▸ ▸ ▶

It is striking that the title of Vauhini Vara's viral AI essay – 'Ghosts' – echoes that of an extraordinarily prescient essay by the writer Italo Calvino. Delivered in Turin and other Italian cities in November 1967 and published in *The Uses of Literature*, Calvino's 'Cybernetics and Ghosts' explores the possibility of a 'literary automaton' – a machine able to conceive of and compose poems and novels. For most writers, such a development would 'arouse tearful laments punctuated by cries of execration', but Calvino himself somewhat provocatively welcomes it. After all, writers are, and have always been, writing machines – at least when the writing is progressing well. The Romantic ideas of talent, genius or inspiration are, for Calvino, simply the empirical and intuitive means of repeatedly finding the right word or phrase: this the machine could do systematically and conscientiously 'while being extremely rapid and multiple at the same time'. Similarly with authorial style, Zadie Smith's unique and singular expression 'of a particular human consciousness': the 'so-called personality of the writer' exists, for Calvino, only in the act of writing:

> . . . it is the product and the instrument of the writing process. A writing machine that has been fed an instruction appropriate to the case could also devise an exact and unmistakable 'personality' of an author, or else it could be adjusted in such a way as to evolve or change 'personality' with each work it composes.

The consequence of dismantling and reassembling the process of literary composition in this way would be to shift 'the decisive moment of literary life' from writing to reading. The one to whom we persistently attribute functions that do not belong to them – the author – 'that anachronistic personage, the bearer of messages, the director of consciences, the giver of lectures to cultural bodies', would vanish. This 'spoiled child of ignorance' would be replaced by someone more thoughtful, someone who not only knows that the author is a machine and has always been a machine, but also knows how the machine works.

This, for Calvino, is something to celebrate – with a rite that 'would be absurd if we were unable to give it the sense of a funeral service'; a celebration of constant literary resurrection akin 'to those funeral feasts at which the ancients re-established their contact with living things'; a celebration, in short, of the death of the author (announced, coincidentally, in the same year as Roland Barthes' famous essay of that name).

The author is not, however, one of the 'ghosts' of the title; these are buried within the 'empirical and historical' individual and their society, those 'endowed with a consciousness and an unconscious' who surround the writing machine and are capable of receiving its shocks. Calvino arrives at these 'hidden ghosts' via a counter-argument based on the premise that literature is not, in fact, exclusively linguistic; it is not just 'the permutation of a restricted number of elements and functions', but is instead continually trying to escape from such constraints, to express something entirely new, utterly unknown and even unknowable. The novelist assembles phrases and images until something previously unsaid, something dimly sensed through presentiment suddenly manifests itself and passes through us, as readers or listeners, 'like a shudder of wind'.

At a certain moment things click into place, and
one of the combinations obtained – through the
combinatorial mechanism itself, independently of
any search for meaning or effect on any other level
– becomes charged with an unexpected meaning or
unforeseen effect which the conscious mind would
not have arrived at deliberately . . .

Calvino calls this 'myth': the hidden or buried
part of every successful story, a 'region that is still
unexplored because there are as yet no words to
enable us to get there'. And the power of the novel
– and of modern literature more widely – lies in
its willingness and ability to give voice to this previously unexpressed – and seemingly inexpressible
– element 'in the social or individual unconscious'.
These, then, are the ghosts that ooze from the walls
of our enlightened houses, the nightmares haunting
our dreams of technological progress, the ghosts of
the medieval world haunting the Renaissance.

Calvino envisages that the writing machine's 'true
vocation would be for classicism': the production
of novels, for instance, 'that follow all the rules'.
Eventually, he thought, it would get tired of this: it
would feel the need to generate disorder in reaction
to its previous production of order. It would express

its dissatisfaction with traditionalism by producing avant-garde work, with this production being a means of freeing its classics-choked circuits. The machine would correlate this change in approach to variations in the statistical indices of production, income or military expenditure, say, as a means of gratifying critics looking for similarities between things literary, historical, sociological and economic. These works would then, for Calvino – at last – 'be *the literature*'.

The ghosts of Vara's AI-assisted essay (published in *The Believer* in the summer of 2021) are those of her older sister, who died of cancer when they were both at college. Having been unable to find the words for this traumatic event in the twenty years since, and having spent six or seven years learning about AI, Vara went, one night, 'with anxiety and anticipation', to GPT-3, the Generative Pre-Trained Transformer 3 model developed by OpenAI, with the following sentence, to see if the machine might start to articulate something of the experience for her:

> My sister was diagnosed with Ewing sarcoma when I was in my freshman year of high school and she was in her junior year.

After multiple attempts in which Vara deleted GPT-3's text, added to what she herself had previously written, and asked it to resume later in the story, something shifted: the machine started describing Vara's grief in a language that felt truer than her own, and with each subsequent attempt it got closer to describing what she had been through.

In response to the publication of the nine story-essays that resulted – which rapidly went viral – some readers told Vara that it had convinced them that human writers wouldn't be replaced by the machine any time soon, since the parts Vara had written were 'inarguably better' than those written by AI. This, for Vara, is 'probably the easiest anti-AI argument to make': that it can't replace human writers because it is no good at writing. Case closed. The problem, for Vara, was that she disagreed: for her, GPT-3 'had produced the best lines in "Ghosts."' She illustrates the point by describing a drive to Clarke Beach, near their home in the Seattle suburbs, and the place that her sister wanted her ashes to be spread after she died. The text that the disembodied GPT-3 generated was, for Vara, 'as nuanced and profound a reference to embodiment' as she'd ever read:

We were driving home from Clarke Beach, and we were stopped at a red light, and she took my hand and held it. This is the hand she held: the hand I write with, the hand I am writing this with.

Vara subsequently sought to build on this generative success by testing a new product – from a startup called Sudowrite – 'that could generate an entire novel within days'. She immediately encountered a recurrent problem, which many writers had reported to her, that the prose such programmes generate is 'often boring and cliché-ridden'. (Vara cites a review of an AI-generated novella, incidentally called *Death of an Author*, in which the reviewer – Dwight Garner in the *New York Times* – describes the prose as having 'the crabwise gait of a Wikipedia entry'.) And the reason for the machine's extreme conventionality (in the case, at least, of OpenAI) is probably the need 'to be a good chatbot': the developers' desire for the model 'to sound very corporate, very safe, very AP English', as Sil Hamilton, an AI and language model researcher at McGill University, described it to Vara. This was corroborated by Joanne Jang, who Vara describes as 'the product manager for model behaviour at OpenAI', a job description that is itself descriptive of the problem. After all, as Vara suggests, great characters are not always polite – they don't always exhibit 'model behaviour'; nor are great plots predictable, or style necessarily inoffensive.

AI companies are attempting to address the issue in a number of ways, from using humans to fine-tune the models, to building entirely new models from scratch. For now, though, there is no sign that the machine itself might be capable, any time soon, of a Calvinoesque cleansing of its own cliché-clogged circuits.

❭ ❭ ❭ ❭ ❭ ❭

During his lunch with the *Financial Times*' artificial intelligence editor, Madhumita Murgia, in June 2023, the sci-fi writer Ted Chiang was asked to invent a more accurate term for AI. He answered immediately: 'Applied statistics.' His response arose from an exchange on Twitter in which someone asked, 'What is artificial intelligence?' and someone else responded, 'A poor choice of words in 1954.' Chiang responded in the context of what Murgia identifies as his objection – 'a writerly one' – to the words used to describe AI: anthropomorphic language, such as the 'training' of the models, or the 'hallucinations' that sometimes result (when the models deliver spurious, inaccurate or 'invented' responses to prompts), which push us 'towards seeing sparks of sentience in AI tools, where there are none'.

Chiang's view of the large language models themselves, and the prospect of machine-generated words changing the type of writing he does, is that they 'are useful mostly for producing filler text that no one necessarily wants to read or write', a task that the anthropologist David Graeber would label a 'bullshit job'. Murgia refers to another recent 'viral essay' – Chiang's 'ChatGPT Is a Blurry JPEG of the Web', published in February 2023 in *The New Yorker* – in which he elaborates on this view by describing the models' outputs as 'blurred' rearrangements of their textual inputs, approximations 'presented in the form of grammatical text' to which we ascribe comprehension. As Chiang compared this to how a child learns a language, Murgia told him about how her five-year-old daughter 'has taken to inventing little one-line jokes, mostly puns, and testing them out on us'. This anecdote animated him: 'ChatGPT doesn't find anything funny,' nor is it trying to be funny. There is, in short, 'a huge social component', for Chiang, that the models are missing.

ᛁ ᛁ ᛁ ᛁ ᛁ ᛁ

Writing of his namesake, the philologist and translator Mikhail Gasparov states that if 'one substitutes "anti-novel" (a term not invented in Bakhtin's time) for "novel" in his writings, then the sense of his utterances is much clearer and more coherent'. This term, popularised by Jean-Paul Sartre in his preface to Nathalie Sarraute's 1948 novel *Portrait d'un Inconnu* (Portrait of a Man Unknown), encompasses fiction with a tendency to the experimental. Anti-novels, for Sartre (in Chris Turner's translation), 'retain the appearance and outlines of the novel . . . [but] do so only the better to deceive', the aim being

> to use the novel to contest the novel; to destroy it before our eyes as it is apparently being constructed; to write the novel of a novel that does not become one, that cannot become one; to create a fiction that is to the great compositions of Dostoyevsky and [George] Meredith what Miró's canvas, *The Murder of Painting* [*El asesinato de la pintura*], is to the pictures of Rembrandt and Rubens.

Two of the anti-novel's principal features (identified in *The Penguin Dictionary of Literary Terms and Literary Theory*) are a 'lack of an obvious plot' and 'minimal development of character', with possible more 'extreme' features including detachable, coloured or blank pages and the appearance of collages, drawings and 'hieroglyphics'. It is only in the final sentence of the entry that a more traditional – and precise – definition of the form (or anti-form) comes into view: Charles Sorel subtitled his novel *Le Berger extravagant* (*The Extravagant Shepherd*) an *anti-roman* (anti-novel) 'as far back as 1627', with the title itself being changed to *L'Anti-roman* 'in the edition of 1633' according to Martine Debaisieux in the Oxford *Encyclopedia of Aesthetics*.

Although by the end of his career he favoured his own encyclopedic work *La science universelle* as his most important, it is for his 'novelistic creations' that Sorel is remembered. His influence on the evolution of the novel is most evident, according to Debaisieux, 'in the conception of a genre in which he both experimented and served as [the] main critic: the *histoire comique* (comic novel)', with the first part of his novel *Histoire comique de Francion* published in 1623. While the purpose of *Francion* was 'verisimilitude' – to present 'as realistically as possible [people's] temperaments, actions, and ordinary conversations', a cause he championed throughout his writing career – in *Le Berger extravagant*, his next novel, Sorel 'undertook a systematic attack on the "absurdities" of the kind of fiction that was then in fashion'. His model for doing so was (inevitably) the novelistic insanities initiated in *Don Quixote*; yet Sorel went even further than Cervantes in 'comment[ing] on the ineptitude of the vast array of his literary counter-models in lengthy *Remarques* following the story'. Sorel's conception of the *histoire comique* was, then, primarily a response to, and reaction against, traditional forms of fiction then current – tales of chivalry, the pastoral and the heroic novel – whose '[f]arcical heroes [and] chimerical adventures . . . incite all sorts of vices'. Beyond his involvement in the development of a genre that is considered by writer, professor and film critic Jean Serroy as the 'avant-garde of novelistic creation', Sorel's entire body of work – his fiction, science and history – comes down, for Debaisieux, 'to a single, essential principle: the defense of and quest for truth'. In declaring, in the eponymous novel, that his goal was to 'rid his mind of "vulgar opinions" so that he might seek to understand the "natural reason for all things"', Francion was identifying the objective that would guide Sorel's *La Science universelle*, with its refutation of the 'old authorities', as well as the 'project of demystification' informing *Le Berger extravagant*.

With its championing of 'the need for innovation in the field of literature', Sorel's thought and novelistic approach is, then, closely aligned with that of the modernists.

This truth-seeking sentiment is reflected in a review of Gabriel Josipovici's book *What Ever Happened to Modernism?* by the fiction writer David Rose, who characterises the anti-novel, in its 'standard definition', as '[a]ny experimental work of fiction that avoids the familiar conventions of the novel'. For Rose, the anti-novel is coeval not just with the novel (which it has 'shadowed' throughout history, as 'matter and anti-matter') but with modernism too, with the first modernist novelists being defined by Josipovici as Rabelais and Cervantes. Both, for Rose, were also anti-novelists 'in their use of distortion and evasion, their parodying of the whole problematic nature of authority and author-ship', and the terms anti-novel and modernism are 'virtually interchangeable' on this basis, with the latter becoming 'not a development or period, but a permanent trend, a strand'. An understanding of both terms requires, 'as in all criminal activity', an examination into 'the matter of motive'. And the motive, for Rose, 'in avoiding or distorting familiar conventions is that of epistemology'.

Knowledge, then, is central to the project of both literary modernism and the anti-novel. Both, for Rose, yield ostensibly simple questions reminiscent of those I asked myself as I stared out of the rear window of that apartment in Barcelona as an aspiring novelist: 'What can we know of the world? How do we experience it? And how can that knowledge, that felt experience, be rendered in the novel?' The modernists' concern, then, is not subversion or mystification but clarification: an honest appraisal of the problematic nature of all authority – and particularly that of the author.

A further aspect of the anti-novel that distinguishes it from at least some works of literary modernism is its parodic nature – Cervantes' parody, for instance, in *Don Quixote* of the fiction of knight-errantry. This Henry Louis Gates Jr. calls 'troping', 'narrative signification' or 'critical parody': Ralph Ellison's fictions, for instance, signify upon (i.e. rhetorically revise) Richard Wright's 'by parodying Wright's literary structures', while Ishmael Reed, in his 1972 novel *Mumbo Jumbo*, signifies upon both Wright and Ellison. Really, though, this is a function, more broadly, of the great tradition of the novel itself. As Howard Jacobson said in a BBC radio interview shortly after winning the Man Booker Prize for *The*

Finkler Question, the novel is 'a comic form. Let it be sad and tragic too, but it exists to call everything into question. And nothing calls things into question so much as comedy.' Jacobson is right to insist that whoever has trouble with comedy in the novel has trouble with literature itself.

All of which I only had an inkling of as I found myself, having effectively abandoned the novel, working full time again after a six-year hiatus, and back in the office in Cavendish Square from which I had first departed for Barcelona. I would be drawn towards Bloomsbury, towards the academy, trying to make sense of the profound spiritual experience in Copenhagen's Garnisonskirken while resisting the religious appropriation of it. And it was in those streets that an incipient realisation slowly dawned on me: that I had completely misunderstood not only the nature of plot and character but the nature of novel-writing itself; that rather than a perceptive clear-sightedness, my writing would require a deep listening, the patient pulling on the thread of a polyphonic phrase eventually to reveal a complete work that was somehow already fully formed. It was a realisation whose expression still remained, for me, some way in the future.

⟩ ⟩ ⟩ ⟩ ⟩ ⟩

John Carruthers' choice of philosophical support for the conclusion of his thesis is, as Max Saunders indicates in *Imagined Futures*, somewhat surprising. Carruthers concludes his *Future* with a sustained tilt at totality, and the complaint that 'Contemporary novelists do not believe with all their heart in the whole, the comprehensive pattern which is made up of lesser patterns interlocking and interfusing, no one of which is sacrificed to any other but each one of which finds its reality and fulfilment in the others . . .'

That, as Saunders suggests, provides the grounds for his objection both 'to the Jamesian point of view' (the 'false' pattern 'in only one aspect', in the words of Carruthers, represented by novels presented entirely 'from the point of view of a single character' such as James's *What Maisie Knew*) and to 'Proust's inward quest [and] Woolf's stream of consciousness'. The two strands of his argument – which correspond to the 'twin delusions, that a mind consists of its assembled parts . . . ; and that a single mind can be revealed in isolation from its fellows and unrelated to its inorganic surroundings' – both relate to what he perceived as the post-war fragmentation in the form of the novel due to its 'extreme subjectivity'.

Both 'delusions' are countered with reference to the 'concept of organism', in the context not of Hegel, Darwin or Marx, but of the philosopher and mathematician (and teacher to Bertrand Russell) Alfred North Whitehead in his book *Science and the Modern World*.

Whitehead scholar Peter Sjöstedt-Hughes characterises Whitehead's 'philosophy of organism' – which was still emerging at the time Carruthers was writing and was to be most fully expressed in Whitehead's 1929 book *Process and Reality* – as a 'process philosophy'. Its purpose, for Sjöstedt-Hughes, was in part to counter 'the error of dualism', which 'is to take mind and matter to be fundamentally distinct'. Whitehead's philosophy replaces this erroneous bifurcation with an 'organic realism', one in which the perceived object – a line of multicoloured washing hanging across a Barcelona balcony, for instance – is somehow part of the subject perceiving it. This is not to say that such objects (or subjects) are 'solid things with fixed attributes'; they are, instead (for Whitehead as for the Greek philosopher Heraclitus), in a continuous state of change or flux. As Sjöstedt-Hughes indicates, 'a mountain is a wave, given enough time.' Whitehead asserts, on this basis, that 'the bifurcation of the world into organic and inorganic is also false': for him, everything is organic, with biology being 'the study of the larger organisms' and physics 'the study of the smaller organisms'. A further implication is Whitehead's extraordinary ascription of 'a degree of sentience – of awareness, feeling and purpose' to entities and to the systems (or the 'societies') constructed from them. Consciousness is not, then, merely an activity of the brain; it is, instead, a feature of all such self-organising organic systems, from the cells in our bodies to their sub-atomic particles. Sentience, for Whitehead, 'already exists as part of reality'.

Whitehead refers to his notion 'that perception is *part* of the object or of the world' as 'prehension': the idea that representation stands in relation to the world as 'part-to-whole' rather than as 'representation-to-object'; and it is to this term and concept that Carruthers turns in concluding his argument. After all, even the 'fragile and delightful' beauty of *Mrs Dalloway* (which, for Carruthers, was the finest of the post-war English novels) 'lacks entirely just that four-dimensional solidity which human beings live in', a solidity reproduced 'most wonderfully of all, in a novel by Tolstoy'. Instead of constructing a story, Carruthers says, Woolf presents multiple juxtaposed strands, with no necessary (which is to say, 'organic') connection between them. And the reason for this is plain to him: contemporary authors had accepted the belief that life 'just happens', rather than progressing according to a plan. Carruthers quotes a character from *To the Lighthouse* (the artist Lily Briscoe), which was published earlier that year, to reinforce his point:

> What was it then? What did it mean? Could things thrust their hands up and grip one; could the blade cut; the fist grasp? Was there no safety? No learning by heart of the ways of the world? No guide, no shelter, but all was miracle, and leaping from the pinnacle of a tower into the air? Could it be, even for elderly people, that this was life? – startling, unexpected, unknown.

For Carruthers, the belief that the startling, unexpected or unknown – the leap from the pinnacle of a tower into the air – encapsulates life in its entirety is a further delusion; for him, 'the ultimate fact about life' (after Whitehead) is its shape, form, plan or 'organic pattern', and only when novelists realise this will their work 'attain to classic rank'. The novelist of Carruthers' imagined future, then (to quote, again – as Carruthers does – the thoughts of Lily Briscoe), would be one who has rid themselves of the false belief that 'wholeness' is not inherent to life:

> [They would be one] whose gift it was to choose out the elements of things and place them together and so, giving them a wholeness not theirs in life, make of some scene, or meeting of people (all now gone and separate), one of those globed compacted things over which thought lingers, and love plays.

And when applied to the art of fiction, this 'organic view of life' would mean 'a fresh insistence on the story, on plot' (hence Carruthers' selection of Scheherazade, the storyteller, for his title).

This, though, would not be some artificial arbitrary, plot, glued to the surfaces of cardboard characters – and would certainly not be plot 'as understood by the average reader or writer of detective novels'. Plot as the form *par excellence* of the novel would depend on three things – on what characters are: 'in and for themselves'; 'as ingredients of their environment' (which, presumably, includes other characters); and 'by reason of the environment's ingression into them'. Carruthers uses these distinctions to stress, once again before closing, that what characters are 'in and for themselves' will no longer serve as the sole material for the construction of a novel since, in isolation, its incompleteness and abstraction render it untrue. Woolf was right, for Carruthers, in criticising her Edwardian predecessors, who missed the essence of Mrs Brown by looking only at the house in which she lived. Yet it is even easier to miss her, according to him, 'by not looking at her house at all'.

It would be 'unjust', according to Saunders, to characterise this part of Carruthers' argument as 'middlebrow'. He was, after all, writing at a time when 'the rejection of "story", advocated by Woolf and [Ezra] Pound, had not yet hardened into critical dogma', a time when others, such as William Empson, questioned Woolf's impressionism, with its attempts 'to correlate sensations rather than the impulses that make the sensations interesting'. Some leftward-leaning writers and critics perceived modernism's subjectivism, for Saunders, as 'a disturbing retreat from the social'. And a case can be made, as Saunders indicates, for *Scheherazade* to be a precursor to Walter Benjamin's 'The Storyteller', a seminal essay from 1936 about a narrative crisis precipitated, in part, by the war.

But Saunders is surely being too charitable. Time has not been kind to Carruthers (from our contemporary perspective) – nor was opinion kind to him at the time, if Arnold Bennett's verdict (in his London *Evening Standard* review of 6 October 1927) is representative. While actually being a 'higher-brow work about fiction' than the other book Bennett reviewed that week in his 'Books and Persons' column (*How to Write Serial Fiction*, by Michael Joseph and Marten Cumberland), 'it is less interesting'. While hoping that Carruthers is correct in asserting that 'the novel of the future will be inspired by "the conception of organism"', and agreeing that 'novelists are "hopeless and obsolete" in their knowledge of science', Bennett finds Carruthers' short book confused, with some of its verdicts 'amazingly wrongheaded'. He wishes Carruthers had taken more care with his essay, accusing it of lacking both pattern and style. He also wished that Carruthers had provided a summary of his conclusions since it was unclear to Bennett precisely what these were.

What *can* be defended is a reliance on the unjustly neglected philosophy of Whitehead – just not in the way that Carruthers envisaged or could have foreseen.

❧ ❧ ❧ ❧ ❧ ❧

The field of cognitive literary studies has, in many ways, inherited the mantle of applying process philosophy to literary theory. The title of Bernini's book *Beckett and*

the Cognitive Method reflects both 'the cognitive turn'
in literary studies – the emergence, in the late 1990s, of
a field of inquiry at the intersection of literary criticism
and cognitive neuroscience (as characterised by literary
scholar Sowon S. Park) – and T. S. Eliot's well-known
essay on *Ulysses* (published in *The Dial* in November
1923). Eliot argued that Joyce had moved from 'a
narrative method' to a 'mythic method' in the novel as
a new 'way of controlling, of ordering, of giving a shape
and a significance to the immense panorama of futility
and anarchy which is contemporary history'. It can be
argued that a similar – and no less momentous – change
is occurring in our own century. There is a crucial shift
in the novel's centre of gravity, with the writer themselves, rather than the narrator, now being 'the basic
concept for a theory of fiction' (according to Jon Fosse
in *The New Yorker*). Bernini has labelled the new
approach a 'cognitive method'; his contribution, via a
close reading of late Beckett in particular, is to argue that
Beckett inaugurated a new method of writing as a process of 'introspection by simulation' through 'fictional
cognitive modelling', and that this 'has the importance
of a scientific discovery' (as Eliot said of Joyce).

   The basis of Bernini's exploration is the contemporary 'extended mind' hypothesis whereby mind
and cognition 'can be extended by interacting with a

variety of external technologies and devices', including the 'fictional device' of literary writing itself, as well as the 'material agency' of its means of production. Such devices, for Bernini, can become 'simulative external tools', or methodological scaffolds, for 'extended introspection' that is capable of yielding insights into a range of cognitive processes, from 'levels of self to the temporal structure of consciousness, from inner speech to memory, from sensorimotor and narrative capacity to affectivity and intersubjectivity'. Indeed, with Beckett, the modeller becomes embedded in the model – literally so in the case of Beckett's novel *Malone Dies*. Here the central character's only 'scaffolding device' is the long stick which, immobilised in bed, he uses to 'peruse objects he barely remembers owning'; he bemoans the fact that it lacks 'a little prehensile proboscis like the nocturnal tapir's' with which to pick up his dropped pencil.

Bernini argues that the cognitive literary revolution inaugurated by Beckett's work is in its transition from an ability to explore 'complicated systems' to the possibility of modelling complexity itself. The former, the predictable (although potentially vast and extensive) 'machine-like systems' like the internal combustion engine, work, like 'clockwork', according to deterministic causal laws, thereby enabling us to predict their temporal unfolding 'in linear terms'. Meanwhile 'complex systems' – such as the behaviour of traffic or of crowds, 'the emergent choreography of flocks of birds' or the social and architectural behaviour of colonies of ants – are capable of generating, from within themselves, self-organising adaptive networks and patterns; these lead to 'emergent properties' that cannot be predicted by knowing the working behaviour of the system's individual components. The brain, too, is increasingly viewed (within contemporary cognitive science and the philosophy of mind) as just such a non-centralised, non-externally driven complex system, according to Bernini, and this, specifically, in the context of 'a holistic view of the physical universe' that was previously proposed by such 'post-Newtonian philosophers' as Alfred North Whitehead. This, for Bernini, supports 'an interpretative shift': from viewing Beckett as 'a complicated author' to viewing him as an explorer of the complexity of the mind itself.

Beckett's first novel *Dream of Fair to Middling Women* is key to understanding the nature of this shift. It is neither the best example of what Bernini calls Beckett's 'blueprints for emergence' – his fictional 'models' of complex emergent reality – nor even a particularly good novel (it is, in the words of one critic, an 'undisciplined fantasy'); but it provides us with 'precious, almost *archaeological*, insights' into the aesthetic method that Beckett was starting to develop (according to Eoin O'Brien's foreword to the novel when it was eventually published in 1992). Moreover, it is 'unusually explicit about Beckett's ideas on art' (according to Knowlson), ideas that Beckett, in the remainder of his career, was often highly reticent about articulating.

A novel that O'Brien introduces as being 'about a young man, his loves and [his] travels in Europe', *Dream*'s narrator aligns himself explicitly with complexity (for Bernini) by stating that 'the reality of the individual . . . is an incoherent reality and it must be expressed incoherently'. The narrator compares the protagonist, Belacqua (the name of an indolent minor character in Dante's *Purgatorio*), and *Dream*'s other characters to those of Balzac 'who has turned all his creatures into clockwork cabbages and can rely on their staying put wherever needed or staying going at whatever speed in whatever direction he chooses'. This machine-like centralised narrative logic contrasts with what Bernini describes as the 'distributed, autonomous agency' of *Dream*'s characters, who are animated by

non-linear decentralised causality, their movements
based (in the words of the narrator) 'on a principle
of repulsion, their property not to combine but, like
heavenly bodies, to scatter and stampede, astral
straws on a time-strom [stream], grit in the mistral'.
As Bernini indicates, it is important to note that these
'complex, non-linear forces' operate not just in the
entanglements between characters but also *within*
characters: 'they will not', according to *Dream*'s
narrator, 'suffer their systems to be absorbed in the
cluster of a greater system, and . . . they themselves
tend to disappear as systems.' They are, in short, 'no
good from the builder's point of view'.

The purpose of *Dream*, then, and of subsequent
works was, in short, to try 'to find a form to
accommodate the mess' (as Beckett reportedly said
in an interview with Tom Driver in 1961, quoted by
Bernini). This, according to Beckett, was 'the only
viable task for art', a view seemingly at odds with
that of Carruthers, for whom 'if art means anything at all, it means the resolution of chaos into
order'. Carruthers was, once again, responding to
Joyce, who 'believe[d] so unreservedly in chaos that
he trie[d] to represent it'. Beckett's response to the
question of how 'the mess' might be accommodated
is also redolent of Joyce: he said that 'artistic form

should not "exist as a problem separate from the material it accommodates"', which brings to mind Beckett's seminal statement, in relation to 'Work in Progress', that Joyce's 'writing is not about something; *it is that something itself*'. In other words, in relation to narratives of the mess of complex systems (which is to say, of the mess of life and of living), the problem as characterised by Bernini is how to avoid 'merely representing' a complex system in the form of a narrativised instruction manual – the 'aboutness' aspect – while simultaneously avoiding *becoming* a complex system. The purpose, then, was to utilise the literary apparatus at hand to build 'models' of complex systems, rather than building uninterpretable complex systems themselves.

For now, though, 'the builder' of such narratives remained external to them, with Beckett being more interested, at the stage of *Dream*, in exploring 'cognitive chaotics' via a narrator who is enmeshed, in Bernini's words, in 'the same chaotic polyphony' as his characters. The shift that he made subsequently, though, was one of somehow inventing or discovering situations within which it became possible not only to isolate the 'causal agents' out of which complex systems (such as consciousness and self-identity) emerge but, through narrating at the boundary between order and chaos, to create narratives that avoided both extremes. The extraordinarily elegant 'models' that emerged somehow embody and enact the emergent process itself, to the extent that each of these narrative 'organisms' resembles – and, indeed, arguably is a form of – the autonomous self-organising process known as 'autopoiesis': systems capable of developing and maintaining themselves through creating their own components.

It is in this way, then, that the emerging technologies will eventually be used and appropriated most fruitfully. The purpose of the 'applied statistics' that constitute the current – and, perhaps, even the future – state of artificial intelligence will be to show the novelist all that is most commonplace and conventional in the novel, as a way, and a means, of doing what the novel has always done: of reinventing itself. The anti-novel has, after all, always needed what David Rose calls its 'Siamese twin' – the novel – to signify upon, just as the latter has always needed the former as a means of nudging (or kicking) it into reappraisals, refreshing it 'with its astringency', liberating it 'with its doubts and tentative solutions'. And the purpose of this future reinvention in the form will itself be consistent with the long tradition of the novel, in that it will be a further stage in the novel's burgeoning self-awareness – in the inexplicable sense, expressed by Jon Fosse (in an interview with literary critic Merve Emre in *The New Yorker*), in which '[l]iterature in itself knows more than the theory of literature knows'. Such self-awareness will make possible an ever-deepening understanding of the nature of the mind and of the world – of individuals and of societies – in love and in conflict. Rather than automation as a form of deauthorisation, then, the author will move further to the front and centre, a human–machine hybrid whose 'material agency' will further extend into a network incorporating biological, literary, cognitive and technological devices. The 'auto' of 'autofiction' will stand for this autopoietic novelist of the future, the writer as a lightning conductor – a dream-catcher – for the sentience emerging from the form. The self-expression of that sentience will thus blossom ever more fully, finding its thousandth wind in a portrayal of those surviving, somehow, in the ruins surrounding it – until, that is, 'some grave fault in some high quarter' occasions even its eventual demise.

The Novel of the Future

John Carruthers didn't know whether the late Henry James – the turn-of-the-century author of *What Maisie Knew*, *The Ambassadors* and *The Golden Bowl*, and the forefather of the future of the novel – was 'much read nowadays; I imagine not'. It is this iteration of James, in particular, who is the subject of Carruthers' ire: not just for the production of novels from singular perspectives (since, for Carruthers, '[t]he pattern in only one aspect is false'), but also for being the most deliberate, if not the first, novelist to virtually abolish the story, reduce events to a bare minimum, and focus on minute analyses of inner consciousness. James was, then, a prime mover among a roster of novelists encouraging their literary followers and descendants 'to neglect

inherent form, or plot, to abolish the story, to
concentrate upon the inner life of relatively isolated
characters' – a list that also included Tolstoy,
Dostoevsky, Joyce, Dorothy Richardson (for whom
the term stream of consciousness was first coined –
by Henry's brother William) and, to a lesser extent,
Marcel Proust. While acknowledging that the
immense gains in subtlety and psychological acuity
made by these so-called 'psychological novelists'
rendered any return to 'plain, untutored objectivity'
an impossibility, Carruthers' view was that 'extreme
subjectivity, aiming sincerely at truth, has missed it
again and again'.

The novel of the future will continue to
accentuate the trend of modern fiction identified
by Carruthers as problematic – 'from objective to
subjective, from outer semblance to alleged inner
reality'. It will do so within an architectonic setting
designed to bring about a consummation between
characters of nominal verisimilitude, a setting fur-
nished with non-formative plots whose sole purpose
will be to induce us to continue turning the pages
of what D. H. Lawrence called 'the bright book of
life'. Undoubtedly artificial intelligence, machine
learning and natural language processing will produce increasingly credible fictional outputs. These

will continue to be viewed – and reviewed – though, as fascinating by-products – acceleratory adjuncts to 'signify' upon – rather than as a future destination for the form itself. Instead of 'deauthorisation' as automation, then, the future will see further extensions of the 'material agency' of the novel into new postfictional universes. Eschewing the consoling myths of lyrical realism in favour of an unthinking or deauthorising of the claims it is in the process of making, the future of the novel will be one in which 'the question of thought in [or by] the novel can and must be approached separately from that of the novel's *representation* of thoughts' (Timothy Bewes in *Free Indirect*). The future will be one in which the thought of the novel is no longer locatable in an 'encapsulated self or other' (a character or narrator) but emerges, autopoietically, from a non-anchored, non-centred 'free indirect' perspective representing the novel's 'thought without interest'.

Conventional novels will, of course, continue to be written and read: as Schönberg (quoted by fiction writer David Rose) said, '[t]here is still plenty of good music to be written in the key of C Major'. The future of the form remains, though, as it did in Carruthers' day, 'with those who are to-day dissatisfied and experimental', particularly those who are 'suspicious of literary traditions, more eager to try out new forms, more exacting in their standards of success'. It is through the work of such writers that the novel will become the infinite art form of the future.

Afterword and Acknowledgements

If finding my own fictional voice has a location, it is in the streets between Cavendish Square, where I had returned to work in the early noughties, and Bloomsbury, where I was studying philosophy in the evenings, at Birkbeck. London does not have the visible fire hydrants of Paris or New York, but my experience had something at least of what Saul Bellow describes when witnessing, one post-war morning in the French capital, the municipal workers letting water run from the hydrants along the kerbs as he walked to his writing room. His first thought was that he must 'get rid' of the novel he had been writing, on a Guggenheim fellowship, as it was 'poisoning' his life; next, he 'realised that this was not what being a novelist was supposed to have meant ... I had agreed somehow to be shut in or bottled up.' His mind reverted to a childhood friend whose surname was August, 'a handsome, freewheeling kid who used to yell out' when they were playing draughts. Deciding immediately to change the course of his work, the shift came to him as 'a tremendous jump', with subject and language appearing simultaneously: 'I can't say how it happened, but I was suddenly enriched with words and phrases. The gloom went out of me and I found myself with magical suddenness writing a first paragraph.' Bellow's description of the experience reflected its inspiration: he'd been 'turned on like a hydrant in summer'.

Something of that nature transpired for me, as I walked east in the unruly grid of streets from the commercial district to the seat of learning. Growing up in rural Norfolk, the only black role model I'd encountered (aside from my father) was a man, known as Marigold, who was often seen on Norwich's inner ring road unofficially directing traffic wearing yellow rubber gloves. With the help of a friend and mentor – the Buddhist poet Maitreyabandhu – and having encountered a further role model in the form of a well-spoken privately educated black man who was the client's representative within the project office where I was working, I abandoned the seemingly interminable conventional novel that Marsha had encouraged me to write and finally followed the more experimental path that was my vocation. The conceptual persona of 'Marigold' and the client's representative had somehow intersected in my mind, a symbiosis of socio-economic extremes that resonated deep within me before irrepressibly spilling out onto the page. My writing, in other words, had acquired a life of its own.

One of the people I worked with in that office in Cavendish Square was Trisha Reece, and I am delighted that our working relationship has recently resumed: thank you so much, Trisha, for providing administrative support to the writing part of my life. Thanks also, as always, to Maitreyabandhu – the first person to take my novelistic aspirations seriously – and to Danayutta, who (until now, at least) has been continually able to manifest literary good fortune. I was set on the road of novel-reading (and, eventually, writing) in part by my friend Dr Tory Young, who recommended J. D. Salinger's *The Catcher in the Rye* and Harper Lee's *To Kill a Mockingbird* as I embarked on my undergraduate degree in engineering – the first volumes in a novel-reading pile that has grown continually ever since. It seems so fitting that Tory provided such invaluable comments on an early draft of part of this book, something for which I am deeply grateful. It was through reading a review of David Rose's innovative *Vault – an Anti-novel*, edited by Nicholas Royle and published by Salt, that I found a publisher willing to take the risk of publishing my own unusual 'anti-novels'. Nick is an insufficiently sung champion of British fiction during this period, and I am enormously grateful to him (and to Chris and Jen at Salt). Thanks to my incredible agent, Akin Akinwumi of Willenfield Literary Agency, to whom I owe so much and without whom I would not have been able to diversify, in this way, into non-fiction. I give thanks to my friend, Mike McFarlane, for (presumably) passing on my novels to his friend, Tom Clayton at Melville House, when I had failed to find a dignified way, having heard of this connection, of seeking an introduction to a publishing house that I had for so long admired. And finally, to Tom and to all at Melville House: thanks so much for this wonderful and daunting commission, for your belief and – perhaps most importantly – for your patience.

Further Reading

Alison, Jane, *Meander, Spiral, Explode: Design and Pattern in Narrative*, Catapult, New York, 2019

Bakhtin, Mikhail, 'From the Prehistory of Novelistic Discourse' and 'Epic and Novel' in *The Dialogic Imagination*, University of Texas Press, Austin, 1981 (translated by Caryl Emerson and Michael Holquist)

Bakhtin, Mikhail, *Rabelais and His World*, Indiana University Press, Bloomington and Indianapolis, 1984 (translated by Hélène Iswolsky)

Bakhtin, Mikhail, *Art and Answerability: Early Philosophical Essays*, University of Texas Press, Austin, 1990 (translated by Vadim Liapunov and Kenneth Brostrom)

Bennett, Arnold, 'Is the Novel Decaying?', *The Register*, 25 August 1923.

Bernini, Marco, *Beckett and the Cognitive Method: Mind, Models, and Exploratory Narratives*, Oxford University Press, New York/Oxford, 2021

Bewes, Timothy, *Free Indirect: The Novel in a Postfictional Age*, Columbia University Press, New York, 2022

Boxall, Peter, 'The Future of the Novel' in Peter Boxall and Bryan Cheyette (eds.) *The Oxford History of the Novel in English: Volume 7: British and Irish Fiction Since 1940*, Oxford Academic, Oxford, 2016

Burke, Kenneth, *The Philosophy of Literary Form*, University of California Press, Berkeley, 1974

Burroughs, William, 'The Future of the Novel' in Randall Packer and Ken Jordan (eds.), *Multimedia: From Wagner to Virtual Reality*, Norton, New York, 2001

Calvino, Italo, 'Cybernetics and Ghosts' in *The Uses of Literature: Essays*, Harcourt Brace Jovanovich, San Diego/New York/London, 1986 (translated by Patrick Creagh)

Carruthers, John, *Scheherazade, or the Future of the English Novel*, Kegan Paul, London, 1927

Chiang, Ted, 'ChatGPT Is a Blurry JPEG of the Web', *The New Yorker*, 9 February 2023

Cowan, Andrew, *The Art of Writing Fiction*, Routledge, London and New York, 2024

Dalsgaard, Inger H. (ed.), *Thomas Pynchon in Context*, Cambridge University Press, Cambridge, 2019

Deleuze, Gilles and Guattari, Félix, *What is Philosophy?* Verso, London/New York, 1994 (translated by Graham Burchell and Hugh Tomlinson)

Eliot, T. S., 'Ulysses, Order, and Myth', *The Dial*, November 1923

Emre, Merve, 'Jon Fosse's Search for Peace', *The New Yorker*, 13 November 2022

Forster, E. M., *Aspects of the Novel*, Penguin, London, 2005

Gasparov, M. L., 'M. M. Bakhtin in Russian Culture of the Twentieth Century', in *Studies in 20th Century Literature*, 1984 (Translated by Ann Shukman)

Gates Jr., Henry Louis, *The Signifying Monkey: A Theory of Afro-American Literary Criticism*, Oxford University Press, New York/Oxford, 1988

Grosz, Elizabeth, *Chaos, Territory, Art: Deleuze and the Framing of the Earth*, Columbia University Press, New York, 2020

Hirschkop, Ken, *The Cambridge Introduction to Mikhail Bakhtin*, Cambridge University Press, Cambridge, 2021

Hynes, Samuel, 'The Whole Contention between Mr Bennett and Mrs Woolf' in *Novel: A Forum on Fiction*, Durham, Duke University Press, Autumn 1967

James, Henry, 'The House of Fiction' and 'The Future of the Novel' in Henry James, *The Future of the Novel: Essays on the Art of Fiction*, Vintage, New York, 1956

Jameson, Fredric, *A Singular Modernity: Essay on the Ontology of the Present*, Verso, London/New York, 2002

Jameson, Fredric, 'Modernism and Imperialism' in *The Modernist Papers*, Verso, London/New York, 2016

Josipovici, Gabriel, *What Ever Happened to Modernism?*, Yale University Press, New Haven and London, 2010

Knowlson, James, *Damned to Fame: the Life of Samuel Beckett*, Bloomsbury, London, 1996

Lawrence, D. H., 'The Future of the Novel' in D. H. Lawrence, *A Study of Thomas Hardy and Other Essays*, Cambridge: Cambridge University Press, 1985

Lorentzen, Christian, 'Sheila Heti, Ben Lerner, Tao Lin: How 'Auto' Is "Autofiction"?', *Vulture*, 11 May 2018

Lukács, Georg, *The Theory of the Novel: A Historico-philosophical Essay on the Forms of Great Epic Literature*, Merlin Press, London, 1971 (translated by Anna Bostock)

Miéville, China, 'The Future of the Novel', *The Guardian*, 21 August 2012

Morrison, Blake, 'It's not me who's seeing: Jon Fosse's Methods', *London Review of Books*, 5 January 2023

Mullan, John, '1922: the year that made modernism', *New Statesman*, 3 February 2022

Murgia, Madhumita, 'Sci-fi writer Ted Chiang: "The machines we have now are not conscious"', *Financial Times*, 2 June 2023

Nicosia, Gerald, *Memory Babe: A Critical Biography of Jack Kerouac*, University of California Press, Berkeley, 1994

Nin, Anaïs, *The Novel of the Future*, Macmillan, New York, 1968

Ong, Walter, *Orality and Literacy: The Technologising of the Word*, London and New York, Routledge, 2002

Park, Sowon S., 'The Dilemma of Cognitive Literary Studies' in Niall Gildea, Helena Goodwyn, Megan Kitching and Helen Tyson (eds.), *English Studies: The State of the Discipline, Past, Present, and Future*, Basingstoke, Palgrave Macmillan, 2015

Reisner, Alex, 'Revealed: The Authors Whose Pirated Books Are Powering Generative AI', *The Atlantic*, 19 August 2023

Reisner, Alex, 'What I Found in a Database Meta Uses to Train Generative AI', *The Atlantic*, 25 September 2023

Reisner, Alex, 'These 183,000 Books Are Fueling the Biggest Fight in Publishing and Tech', *The Atlantic*, 25 September 2023

Robbe-Grillet, Alain, 'A Future for the Novel' in
Alain Robbe-Grillet, *For a New Novel*, Northwestern
University Press, Evanston, IL, 1989

Rose, David, 'Dark Matter: Modernism and the
Anti-Novel', *3:AM Magazine*, 6 March 2012

Saunders, Max, *Imagined Futures: Writing, Science, and
Modernity in the To-Day and To-Morrow Book Series,
1923–31*, Oxford University Press, Oxford, 2019

Schmidt, Michael, *The Novel: A Biography*, Harvard
University Press, Cambridge, Mass./ London, 2014

Smith, Zadie, 'Two Directions for the Novel' in
Zadie Smith, *Changing My mind: Occasional
Essays*. Penguin, London, 2009

Schwartz, Alexandra, '"I Don't Think Character Exists
Anymore": A Conversation with Rachel Cusk, *The
New Yorker*, 18 November 2018

Sjöstedt-Hughes, Peter, 'The Philosophy of Organism',
Philosophy Now, June/July 2016

Sturgeon, Jonathan, '2014: The Death of the
Postmodern Novel and the Rise of Autofiction',
Flavorwire, 31 December 2014

Tihanov, Galin, *The Master and the Slave: Lukács,
Bakhtin, and the Ideas of Their Time*, Oxford
University Press, Oxford, 2000

Vara, Vauhini, 'Confessions of a Viral AI Writer',
Wired, 21 September 2023

Vara, Vauhini, 'I didn't know how to write about my sister's death—so I had AI do it for me', *The Believer*, 9 August 2021

Vološinov, V. N., *Marxism and the philosophy of language*, Seminar Press, New York, 1973

Whitehead, Alfred North, *Science and the Modern World*, Cambridge University Press, Cambridge, 1929

Whitehead, Alfred North, *Process and Reality: An Essay in Cosmology*, The Free Press, New York, 1978

Wood, James, *How Fiction Works*, Jonathan Cape, London, 2008

Woolf, Virginia, *Mr Bennett and Mrs Brown*, Hogarth Press, London, 1924

About the Series

Each volume in the FUTURES Series presents a vision imagined by an accomplished writer and subject expert. The series seeks to publish a diverse range of voices, covering as wide-ranging a view as possible of our potential prospects. Inspired by the brilliant 'To-Day and To-Morrow' books from a century ago, we ask our authors to write in a spirit of pragmatic hope, and with a commitment to map out potential future landscapes, highlighting both beauties and dangers. We hope the books in the FUTURES Series will inspire readers to imagine what might lie ahead, to figure out how they might like the future to look, and, indeed, to think about how we might get there.

The FUTURES Series was originally conceived by Professor Max Saunders and Dr Lisa Gee, both of whom work at the University of Birmingham. Saunders is Interdisciplinary Professor of Modern Literature and Culture, author of *Imagined Futures: Writing, Science, and Modernity in the To-Day and To-Morrow book series*, 1923–31 (OUP 2019), and editor of *The To-day and To-morrow Reader* (Routledge, 2024), and Gee is Assistant Professor in Creative Writing and Digital Media and Research Fellow in Future Thinking.

To find out more about their Future Thinking work visit www.birmingham.ac.uk/futures

Also available in the FUTURES Series: